Betty Crocker's

Vegetarian COOKING

*Easy Meatless Main Dishes
Your Family Will Love!*

Hungry Minds, Inc.

Hungry Minds, Inc.
909 Third Avenue
New York, NY 10022

Hungry Minds is a registered trademark of Hungry Minds, Inc.
BETTY CROCKER and BISQUICK are registered trademarks of General Mills, Inc.
Library of Congress Cataloging-in-Publication Data
Crocker, Betty.
    Betty Crocker's vegetarian cooking : easy meatless main
dishes your family will love. — 1st ed.
        p.   cm.
    ISBN 0-02-862261-8
    1. Vegetarian cookery.   I. Title
TX837.C782   1998
641.5'636—dc21   97-32222
                                                                        CIP

GENERAL MILLS, INC.
Betty Crocker Kitchens
Director: Marcia Copeland
Editor: Lori Fox
Recipe Development: Altanette Autry, Nancy Cooper, Grace Wells
Food Stylist: Cindy Lund
Nutritionists: Elyse A. Cohen, M.S., Nancy Holmes, R.D.
Photographer: Carolyn Immel

Cover design: George J. McKeon
Book design: George J. McKeon

For consistent baking results, the Betty Crocker Kitchens
recommends Gold Medal flour.

Manufactured in the United States of America
10 9 8 7 6 5 4

First edition
Cover photo: Lasagna Primavera (page 213)
Back cover photos: Oriental Wild Rice Soup (page 17),
Roasted Vegetable Wraps with Garlic Mayonnaise (page 60), Pesto-
Eggplant Sandwiches (page 62), Spinach Pasta Salad (page 96)

Introduction

More and more of us want vegetarian meals; some are interested in eating less red meat and pumping up vegetables, grains, beans and pasta, while others choose a completely vegetarian diet. If you're like many families, you might have both types pulling a chair up to the dinner table!

Betty Crocker has created this book for the wide diversity of vegetarian eaters, showing just how versatile—and easy—vegetarian meals can be. These hearty, family-pleasing recipes put to rest the myth that vegetarian food is "weird" or that you have to drive to out-of-the-way stores to find the ingredients you need.

And to make it even easier on cooks in families where some members are full-time vegetarians and others are occasional vegetarians, many of the recipes show how to add chicken, fish or seafood. You can make the recipe for your full-time vegetarian, then, for example, add slices of grilled chicken or boiled shrimp for the rest of the family. Look for these easy "add-ins" at the end of recipes.

Starting with Hearty Soups, Stews and Chilies, dig into Vegetable Chowder in Bread Bowls and Three-Alarm Spaghetti and Pinto Bean Chili. Go for it with our Satisfying Sandwiches and Pizzas—Roasted Vegetable Wraps with Garlic Mayonnaise and Niçoise French Bread Pizza are just a few of the great tastes. Explore your adventurous side with Meal-Sized Salads such as Autumn Harvest Salad and Caramelized-Vegetable Salad.

Easy Skillet Meals can't be beat on busy nights—whip up Vegetable Curry with Couscous or Fresh Spinach and New Potato Frittata. Looking for simple One-Dish Oven Meals? Try Onion and Cheese Pie or Spaghetti Basil Torte. Finally, add a little spunk with our Simple Side Dishes and Breads, such as Artichoke-Rosemary Bruschetta or Fettuccine and Broccoli with Sharp Cheddar Sauce.

Want to learn more about vegetarian lingo and the best ingredients to have on hand? Then check out the glossary of vegetarian cooking terms and read about how to stock a vegetarian pantry. And, to help you get in the swing of vegetarian cooking, we have included 14 easy meatless menus to cover a variety of occasions.

So, whether you are a full-time vegetarian looking for new ideas, an occasional vegetarian who wants easy recipes with familiar ingredients or someone who just wants good food, you'll find everything you need in *Betty Crocker's Easy Everyday Vegetarian.*

Betty Crocker's

Contents

The Everyday Vegetarian

Vegetarianism, or simply including more meatless meals in our everyday diet, have both become more popular. Some people have selected to omit all meat and animal by-products from their diet for health or ethical reasons. Others have selected to omit only meat for health or economical reasons. Many of us are increasing the amount of vegetables, fruits, grains and legumes in our diets and therefore are eating more meatless meals.

Whichever type of vegetarian you may be, you will find recipes in this book that are easy and tasty for your everyday cooking and eating. The recipes do not include meat, poultry, fish or seafood. However, we have included poultry, fish, seafood, or turkey ham or sausage variations with some of the recipes for those who select to include those foods in their diet.

VEGETARIAN BENEFITS: HEALTH AND NUTRITION

What we eat has the potential to promote or harm us, depending upon our specific food choices. Adopting a vegetarian way of eating, namely diets that are low in fat and saturated fat and high in fiber, has been shown to provide health and nutrition benefits.

Many vegetarians often adopt a healthful lifestyle in addition to dietary changes that may help to decrease the risk of disease. Vegetarian practices often reflect choices of not smoking, refraining from or moderate usage of alcoholic beverages, participating in regular exercise, getting adequate rest and sleep, monitoring health and well-being, and actively seeking help or treatment for health problems.

Strong research data support that vegetarians are at less risk for the following disorders: obesity, constipation, lung cancer, alcoholism, high blood pressure, heart disease, Type II (adult-onset) diabetes and gallstones. Some data support a reduced risk of breast cancer, diverticular disease, colon cancer, kidney stones (calcium), osteoporosis, dental erosion and dental cavities.

Reduced risk of certain diseases indeed may be due to a combination of both lifestyle and dietary practices. More studies are necessary to determine the true benefits for vegetarians and whether they can translate to the entire U.S. population.

VERSATILE VEGETARIANS

Many people call themselves vegetarians, yet each can sit down to a meal that is extremely different. How vegetarians choose to eat is a matter of choice, and there is great variety from which to choose. Some popular styles of vegetarianism are described below.

Ovo-Lacto Vegetarian

This is the most popular style of vegetarianism in the United States. The main reason for selecting this style is for health. The diet includes eggs (ovo) and dairy products (lacto), but eliminates meat, poultry, fish and seafood. This diet provides a wide variety of food selections, so eating away from home seldom is a problem.

DO EAT: Vegetables, fruits, grains, legumes, nuts, seeds, eggs and dairy products such as milk and milk-based foods.

DO NOT EAT: Meat, poultry, fish or seafood. May not eat animal-based broths such as chicken, beef, fish or seafood.

Lacto-Vegetarian

This is probably the most popular style worldwide because it is the traditional East Indian diet. Many people select it because they are cutting eggs from their diet due to cholesterol or to avoid allergic reaction.

DO EAT: Vegetables, fruits, grains, legumes, nuts, seeds and dairy products such as milk and milk-based foods.

DO NOT EAT: Eggs, meat, poultry, fish or seafood. May not eat animal-based broths such as chicken, beef, fish or seafood.

Vegan Vegetarian

This is the most strict style of vegetarianism because the diet includes no animal products or by-products. A main reason why someone might choose this style of vegetarianism is for ethical reasons. It is more difficult to eat away from home when following a vegan diet.

DO EAT: Vegetables, fruits, grains, legumes, nuts and seeds.

DO NOT EAT: Meat, poultry, fish or seafood, eggs, dairy products such as milk and milk-based foods or products containing animal products such as chicken, beef, fish or seafood broth, lard or gelatin. Vegans may not use animal products or animal by-products such as honey, leather, fur, silk, wool, cosmetics or soaps.

Semi-Vegetarian

This is a term that has become very trendy although some may not view it as a legitimate style of vegetarianism. It often refers to people who include more meatless meals in their diet but who still occasionally eat fish, poultry and meat. Or it may be those who eat fish and poultry but who have eliminated meat from their diet. Overall, even though it might be a controversial form of vegetarianism, people eating this way are including more vegetables, fruits, grains and legumes to their diet, which is a more healthful lifestyle. This generally does not create problems for selecting foods when eating away from home.

DO EAT: Vegetables, fruits, grains, legumes, nuts, seeds, eggs and dairy products such as milk and milk-based foods. May include poultry, fish and seafood but usually limit these foods to occasional use.

DO NOT EAT: Usually avoid red meat.

Mom, I Want to Be a Vegetarian!

Teens make up the fastest-growing segment of the U.S. population that is interested in becoming or choosing to become vegetarians. This style of eating usually is explored for ethical or environmental reasons, but in some cases, especially with young women, it can be to lose weight.

Panic is often the first reaction nonvegetarian parents have when teens make this announcement. Nutrition and meal planning are primary concerns, after all, and this is brand-new territory! The key to a healthful, successful vegetarian diet is variety.

Fear not, the majority of vegetarian diets are healthful and incorporate the principles of the U.S. Department of Agriculture (USDA) and U.S. Department of Health and Human Services (USD-HHS) Food Guide Pyramid with its emphasis on eating plenty of grains, legumes, vegetables and fruit. And with some minor alterations, only one family meal needs to be made rather than cooking separate, highly specialized meals for your vegetarian teens.

Encourage your teens to come up with ideas for their own recipe creations, and allow them to shop for the ingredients and prepare the recipe for the family. If your teens are very strict about what they eat, they may want to help prepare their own part of the family meal. Allowing that type of initiative and creativity to shine through will make the transition to vegetarianism easier for everyone.

NUTRITION GUIDELINES

Most teenagers' diets could use a bit of fine tuning, and because teens are still growing, they require extra nutrients and calories. Here are some nutrition guidelines to follow to ensure a healthy vegetarian diet:

Protein

The fact is, American meat eaters are getting more protein than they need. Eliminating meat protein from your diet will decrease protein intake, but vegetarian diets usually meet or even exceed the Recommended Dietary Allowance (RDA). The recommended amounts of protein are 44 grams for girls 15 to 18 years old, 59 grams for boys 15 to 18 years old, 50 grams for adult women and 63 grams for adult men. Recent studies confirm that as long as you eat a variety of foods each day, you'll most likely eat enough protein to meet your needs. Vegetarians not eating protein from animal sources rely on protein found in combinations of legumes, grains, pastas, cereals, breads, nuts and seeds. Read more about the myths of protein on page 10.

Vitamin B_{12}

Vitamin B_{12} is necessary for all body cells to function properly. It occurs naturally only in animal foods but can be found in supplements. Vegans are the only vegetarians who need to supplement their diets with B_{12}. A B_{12} deficiency can lead to anemia and nerve damage.

Iron

Teenage girls, and women in general, even nonvegetarians, have some difficulty getting enough iron in their diets. The RDA for iron for adult women is 18 milligrams. Taking an iron supplement is the best way to get the iron you need if you are not eating any animal-source foods. Nonanimal iron sources are absorbed more easily by the body when eaten with vitamin C, such as in an orange or orange juice.

Calcium

Teenage girls, and women in general, even nonvegetarians, have difficulty getting enough calcium in their diets. Before the age of 25, the RDA for calcium is 1,200 milligrams, and for those over the age of 25, the RDA is 800 milligrams.

If you take a calcium supplement, follow these three guidelines to get the most out of this nutrient:

1. Limit doses to 600 milligrams at one time, so the body can absorb it more easily.

2. Take it with meals, to help with absorption.

3. If not taking multivitamins, look for calcium tablets containing vitamin D, which helps with absorption.

13 Best Non-Animal Iron Sources

Food	Amount	Iron (milligrams)
Ready-to-eat cereals (fortified)	1 cup	4.5 to 8.1
Quinoa	1 cup cooked	5.3
Spinach	1 cup cooked	4.0
Black-eyed peas	1/2 cup cooked	3.8
Lentils	1/2 cup cooked	3.4
Swiss chard	1 cup cooked	3.2
Lima beans	1/2 cup cooked	2.9
Prunes	10 dried	2.4
Blackstrap molasses	1 tablespoon	2.3
Millet	1 cup cooked	2.2
Raisins	1/2 cup	1.7
Winter squash (acorn, buttercup, butternut, Hubbard)	1 cup cooked	1.4
Brewer's yeast	1 tablespoon	1.4

15 Best Calcium Sources

Food	Amount	Calcium (milligrams)
Milk (skim and low-fat)	1 cup	300
Tofu (calcium-fortified)	1/2 cup	258
Yogurt	1 cup	250
Orange juice (calcium-fortified)	1 cup	240
Ready-to-eat cereals (calcium-fortified)	1 cup	200
Mozzarella cheese (part-skim)	1 ounce	183
Canned salmon with bones	3 ounces	181
Collards	1/2 cup cooked	179
Ricotta cheese (part-skim)	1/4 cup	169
Bread (calcium-fortified)	2 slices	160
Cottage cheese (1 percent fat)	1 cup	138
Parmesan cheese	2 tablespoons grated	138
Navy beans	1 cup cooked	128
Turnips	1/2 cup cooked	125
Broccoli	1 cup cooked	94

MYTHS ABOUT VEGETARIANISM

MYTH: I HAVE TO EAT WEIRD FOODS!

FACT: You've probably been eating meatless or vegetarian for a long time but just didn't think of it that way. Take a look at the vegetarian foods most of us are used to! Favorites include cheese or vegetable pizza, grilled cheese sandwiches, spaghetti with tomato sauce, vegetable omelets, macaroni and cheese, peanut butter and jelly sandwiches, cheese quesadillas or pasta primavera. They all qualify as a style of vegetarian eating.

MYTH: I WON'T GET ENOUGH PROTEIN.

FACT: Meatless foods can provide enough protein for the growth and maintenance of body tissues.

Proteins are made of building blocks called *amino acids.* Some of these amino acids we can make in our bodies. The amino acids we cannot produce, called *essential amino acids,* must come directly from the foods we eat.

Proteins that contain all our essential amino acids, called *complete* or *high-quality* proteins, come from animal sources such as meat, eggs, chicken, fish and dairy products. Non-animal protein sources, such as legumes, grains, pastas, cereals, breads, nuts and seeds, are *incomplete* or *lower-quality* proteins because the protein they provide is missing at least one of the essential amino acid building blocks.

MYTH: I MUST EAT LOWER-QUALITY PROTEINS TOGETHER TO GET THE ESSENTIAL AMINO ACIDS I NEED.

FACT: Complementary protein foods do not have to be eaten at the same meal for you to reap the benefits of complete protein! Recent studies show that as long as you eat a variety of foods every day, you'll get enough complete protein to meet your needs.

To ensure we eat good-quality protein, we can combine lower-quality proteins. This way, lower-quality protein foods can complement or complete the amino acids missing from one another to create complete protein with equal quality to animal protein.

Grain foods complement legumes; legumes complement nuts or seeds. The pairings are almost endless. Familiar examples of high-quality protein include peanut butter on whole wheat bread and a bean burrito (beans in a corn tortilla). By eating a lower-quality protein food, such as pasta, with a high-quality protein, such as cheese, you can complete the protein.

MYTH: I WILL HAVE TO EAT MUSHY, BLAND MEALS.

FACT: Variety is the key to any diet, and a variety of foods offer different tastes, color and texture to your meals. Sprinkle toasted nuts or seeds on a salad or casserole for added pizzazz. Go on an adventure using herbs and spices, flavored vinegars, condiments, and fresh citrus juice or peel. A dash of vinegar or lemon juice added just before serving a legume soup provides a kick of flavor. Cook vegetables just until they are tender or crisp-tender for texture, and sprinkle with chopped fresh herbs.

MYTH: I WILL HAVE TO SPEND MORE TIME AND MONEY IF I BECOME A VEGETARIAN.

FACT: Anything new takes a little extra attention, but once you're used to this new way of eating, it will be easier. Years ago, eating vegetarian might have been more difficult, but today it has become more mainstream. Many supermarkets carry a wide variety of vegetarian foods, both on the shelf and in the refrigerator and freezer sections. The number of natural or co-op stores has increased (see page 98). Many vegetables, grains, legumes and nut products are less expensive per pound than meat, poultry, fish and seafood, so a vegetarian diet can be very easy on your budget.

MYTH: I CAN EAT ONLY SALADS AT RESTAURANTS.

FACT: More and more restaurants offer vegetarian entrées on their menus. In addition, many restaurants now prepare many dishes to order, so you can request that the meat portion of the dish be omitted. Many ethnic restaurants, such as Mexican, Middle Eastern and Asian, have vegetarian options because these dishes are part of their traditional diet. Be creative as you check the menu. The appetizer section often offers meatless choices that you can make into a meal by picking a couple of them. Or combine an appetizer with a few vegetable side dishes. Also, if you don't see anything that you can eat, ask your server if he or she can make a suggestion for you.

MYTH: I HAVE TO BE YOUNG TO BECOME A VEGETARIAN.

FACT: It is no longer the diet for just the young and rebellious, as it was viewed in the 1960s. More older people are turning to a vegetarian diet, or reducing meat and animal by-products, because of health concerns. Many are combating weight gain, higher cholesterol and blood pressure, increased cancer risk and digestion problems.

1

Hearty Soups, Stews and Chilies

Oriental Wild Rice Soup
(page 17)

Minestrone

PREP: 20 min; COOK: 20 min

4 SERVINGS

Pesto is delicious on this hearty soup, but if it isn't available, shredded Parmesan cheese can be sprinkled on top.

1 tablespoon olive or vegetable oil

1 large onion, coarsely chopped (1 cup)

1 medium green bell pepper, coarsely chopped (1 cup)

2 cans (14 1/2 ounces each) ready-to-serve vegetable broth

2 cans (14 1/2 ounces each) Italian-style stewed tomatoes with garlic, oregano and basil, undrained

1 can (15 to 16 ounces) dark red kidney beans, rinsed and drained

1 medium yellow summer squash or zucchini, cut lengthwise in half, then cut crosswise into slices (1 1/2 cups)

1 cup uncooked small pasta shells (4 ounces)

1/4 cup pesto

Shredded Parmesan cheese, if desired

1. Heat oil in 3-quart saucepan over medium-high heat. Cook onion and bell pepper in oil 3 to 5 minutes, stirring occasionally, until crisp-tender.

2. Stir in broth, tomatoes and beans. Heat to boiling; reduce heat to medium-low. Simmer uncovered 5 minutes.

3. Stir in squash and pasta. Heat to boiling. Boil 8 to 10 minutes, stirring occasionally, until pasta is tender. Top each serving with pesto; swirl in slightly. Garnish with shredded Parmesan cheese.

1 Serving: Calories 355 (Calories from Fat 115); Fat 13g (Saturated 3g); Cholesterol 2mg; Sodium 1600mg; Carbohydrate 54g (Dietary Fiber 8g); Protein 13g.

CHICKEN MINESTRONE: *Add 1 cup cubed cooked chicken or turkey with the pasta in step 3. Continue as directed.*

Tex-Mex Vegetable Soup

PREP: 4 min; COOK: 12 min

5 SERVINGS

There are two types of ground chilies available. One is strictly ground chilies with nothing else added; it's quite spicy. Chili powder is a blend, containing ground chilies and other spices such as cumin, oregano, garlic, coriander and cloves, and is milder.

1 package (16 ounces) frozen garlic-seasoned pasta, broccoli, corn and carrots

1 jar (16 ounces) thick-and-chunky salsa (2 cups)

1 can (15 ounces) black beans, rinsed and drained

1 can (2 1/4 ounces) sliced ripe olives, drained

2 cups water

1 teaspoon chili powder

1 cup shredded Cheddar or Monterey Jack cheese (4 ounces)

Sour cream, if desired

1. Mix all ingredients except cheese and sour cream in 4-quart Dutch oven. Heat to boiling; reduce heat to low. Simmer uncovered 5 to 7 minutes, stirring occasionally, until vegetables are tender.

2. Top each serving with cheese and sour cream.

1 Serving: Calories 320 (Calories from Fat 125); Fat 14g (Saturated 6g); Cholesterol 30mg; Sodium 960mg; Carbohydrate 43g (Dietary Fiber 10g); Protein 16g.

Beer and Cheese Soup

PREP: 10 min; COOK: 15 min

5 SERVINGS

2 tablespoons margarine or butter

1 large onion, chopped (1 cup)

2 medium carrots, finely chopped (1 cup)

1 medium stalk celery, finely chopped (1/2 cup)

1/4 cup all-purpose flour

1 can or bottle (12 ounces) beer*

2 cups vegetable or chicken broth

1/2 teaspoon salt

1 cup low-fat sour cream

2 cups shredded reduced-fat sharp Cheddar cheese (8 ounces)

1. Melt margarine in 3-quart saucepan over medium heat. Cook onion, carrots and celery in margarine, stirring occasionally, until tender.

2. Stir in flour. Gradually stir in beer, broth and salt. Heat to boiling; reduce heat to low. Cover and simmer about 10 minutes or until vegetables are tender.

3. Remove saucepan from heat. Stir in sour cream and cheese; continue stirring until cheese is melted.

*1 1/2 cups vegetable or chicken broth can be substituted for the beer.

1 Serving: Calories 290 (Calories from Fat 145); Fat 16g (Saturated 8g); Cholesterol 40mg; Sodium 990mg; Carbohydrate 22g (Dietary Fiber 2g); Protein 17g

Tortellini Soup

PREP: 12 min; COOK: 25 min

5 SERVINGS

Next to the ever-popular chicken and beef bouillon granules, you will now find vegetable granules. These granules are a convenient way to add great flavor in a flash! They're also a must for people who don't want to use any animal products.

2 tablespoons margarine or butter

1 small onion, chopped (1/4 cup)

1 medium stalk celery, chopped (1/2 cup)

1 medium carrot, chopped (1/2 cup)

1 clove garlic, finely chopped

6 cups water

4 teaspoons vegetable or chicken bouillon granules

1 package (10 ounces) dried cheese-filled tortellini

1 tablespoon chopped fresh parsley

1/2 teaspoon ground nutmeg

1/4 teaspoon pepper

Freshly grated Parmesan cheese, if desired

1. Melt margarine in 4-quart Dutch oven over medium heat. Cook onion, celery, carrot and garlic in margarine, stirring frequently until crisp-tender.

2. Stir in water and bouillon granules. Heat to boiling; reduce heat to low. Stir in tortellini. Cover and simmer about 20 minutes, stirring occasionally, until tortellini are tender.

3. Stir in parsley, nutmeg and pepper. Sprinkle each serving with cheese.

1 Serving: Calories 145 (Calories from Fat 70); Fat 8g (Saturated 3g); Cholesterol 50mg; Sodium 1110mg; Carbohydrate 14g (Dietary Fiber 1g); Protein 5g.

Brown Rice and Vegetable Cheese Soup

PREP: 5 min; COOK: 10 min

4 SERVINGS

Unlike white rice, in which the germ and bran have been "polished off," brown rice retains these coatings, giving it a nutlike flavor and chewy texture. In addition, brown rice is a good source of fiber and thiamin.

4 ounces process cheese spread loaf, cubed

3 1/2 cups milk

1/2 teaspoon ground mustard (dry)

2 cups cooked brown or white rice

1 package (16 ounces) frozen cauliflower, carrots and asparagus, thawed and drained

1. Heat cheese and milk in 3-quart saucepan over low heat, stirring occasionally, until cheese is melted.

2. Stir in mustard. Stir in rice and vegetables; cook until hot.

1 Serving: Calories 340 (Calories from Fat 125); Fat 14g (Saturated 9g); Cholesterol 45mg; Sodium 550mg; Carbohydrate 39g (Dietary Fiber 4g); Protein 18g.

Oriental Wild Rice Soup

This light soup is bursting with flavor! Complete the meal by serving it with a crusty whole grain or sourdough bread.

1/2 cup uncooked wild rice

3 cups water

1 small red bell pepper, chopped (1/2 cup)

1 can (14 1/2 ounces) ready-to-serve
    vegetable broth

1 1/2 cups sliced mushrooms (4 ounces)

1 1/2 cups 1/2-inch pieces Chinese pea pods

3 tablespoons soy sauce

1/4 teaspoon garlic powder

1/4 teaspoon ground ginger

Chopped fresh cilantro, if desired

1. Heat wild rice and water to boiling in 3-quart saucepan; reduce heat to low. Cover and simmer 45 minutes, stirring occasionally.

2. Stir in bell pepper and broth. Cook uncovered over medium heat 5 minutes, stirring occasionally.

3. Stir in remaining ingredients except cilantro. Cook uncovered over medium heat 5 to 8 minutes, stirring occasionally, until vegetables are crisp-tender. Sprinkle each serving with cilantro.

1 Serving: Calories 120 (Calories from Fat 10); Fat 1g (Saturated 0g); Cholesterol 0mg; Sodium 1210mg; Carbohydrate 25g (Dietary Fiber 3g); Protein 6g.

ORIENTAL CHICKEN AND WILD RICE SOUP: *Add 1 cup diced cooked chicken or turkey with remaining ingredients in step 3. Continue as directed.*

Minnesota Wild Rice Soup

PREP: 15 min; COOK: 25 min

5 SERVINGS

Wild rice isn't actually a rice but rather an aquatic grass native to North America. While its chewy texture makes it a perfect meat substitute, cooked white or brown rice can be used instead of the wild rice. To reduce the fat and calories in this recipe, try nonfat half-and-half and reduce the almonds to 1/4 cup.

2 tablespoons margarine or butter

2 medium stalks celery, sliced (1 cup)

1 medium carrot, coarsely shredded (1/2 cup)

1 medium onion, chopped (1/2 cup)

1 small green bell pepper, chopped (1/2 cup)

3 tablespoons all-purpose flour

1/2 teaspoon salt

1/4 teaspoon pepper

1 1/2 cups cooked wild rice

1/2 cup water

1 can (14 1/2 ounces) ready-to-serve vegetable or chicken broth

1 cup half-and-half

1/3 cup slivered almonds, toasted*

1/4 cup chopped fresh parsley

1. Melt margarine in 3-quart saucepan over medium heat. Cook celery, carrot, onion and bell pepper in margarine, stirring occasionally, until celery is tender.

2. Stir in flour, salt and pepper. Stir in wild rice, water and broth. Heat to boiling; reduce heat to low. Cover and simmer 15 minutes, stirring occasionally.

3. Stir in remaining ingredients. Heat just until hot (do not boil).

*To toast nuts in the microwave, mix nuts and 1 teaspoon margarine or butter, melted, in shallow microwavable bowl or pie plate. Microwave uncovered on High, stirring every 30 seconds, until light brown: 1/4 cup nuts 1 1/2 to 2 minutes, 1/2 cup nuts 2 1/2 to 3 minutes or 1 to 1 1/2 cups nuts 3 to 4 minutes.

1 Serving: Calories 235 (Calories from Fat 125); Fat 14g (Saturated 5g); Cholesterol 20mg; Sodium 680mg; Carbohydrate 24g (Dietary Fiber 3g); Protein 6g.

Tortilla Soup

PREP: 8 min; COOK: 25 min

4 SERVINGS

Stale tortillas are used in many ways by Mexican cooks and never wasted. Feel free to use your stale, or fresh, tortillas. Sliced and fried, they add a distinctive flavor to this tomato soup.

2 teaspoons vegetable oil

4 corn tortillas (5 or 6 inches in diameter), cut into 2 × 1/2-inch strips

1 teaspoon vegetable oil

1 medium onion, chopped (1/2 cup)

2 cans (14 1/2 ounces each) ready-to-serve vegetable or chicken broth

1 can (10 ounces) chopped tomatoes and green chilies, undrained

1 tablespoon lime juice

1 tablespoon chopped fresh cilantro or parsley

1. Heat 2 teaspoons oil in 2-quart nonstick saucepan over medium-high heat. Cook tortilla strips in oil 30 to 60 seconds, stirring occasionally, until crisp and light golden brown. Remove from saucepan; drain on paper towels.

2. Add 1 teaspoon oil and the onion to saucepan. Cook over medium-high heat, stirring occasionally, until onion is tender.

3. Stir in broth and tomatoes. Heat to boiling; reduce heat to low. Simmer uncovered 20 minutes.

4. Stir in lime juice. Serve soup over tortilla strips. Garnish with cilantro.

1 Serving: Calories 190 (Calories from Fat 70); Fat 8g (Saturated 2g); Cholesterol 25mg; Sodium 1230mg; Carbohydrate 20g (Dietary Fiber 2g); Protein 12g.

CHICKEN TORTILLA SOUP: *Cut 2 boneless, skinless chicken breast halves (about 8 ounces) into 3/4-inch pieces. Cook in step 2 with onion 5 minutes or until chicken is no longer pink in center. Continue as directed.*

Lentil-Vegetable Soup

PREP: 10 min; COOK: 40 min

6 SERVINGS

1 large onion, chopped (1 cup)

2 teaspoons chili powder

1 teaspoon salt

1 teaspoon ground cumin

2 cloves garlic, finely chopped

1 can (5.5 ounces) spicy tomato juice

3 cups water

1 cup dried lentils (8 ounces), sorted and rinsed

1 can (14 1/2 ounces) whole tomatoes, undrained

1 can (4 ounces) chopped green chilies, undrained

1 cup fresh or frozen whole kernel corn

2 small zucchini, cut into julienne strips (2 cups)

1. Heat onion, chili powder, salt, cumin, garlic and tomato juice to boiling in 3-quart saucepan; reduce heat to low. Cover and simmer 5 minutes.

2. Stir in water, lentils, tomatoes and chilies, breaking up tomatoes. Heat to boiling; reduce heat to low. Cover and simmer 20 minutes.

3. Stir in corn. Cover and simmer 10 minutes. Stir in zucchini. Cover and simmer about 5 minutes or until lentils and zucchini are tender.

1 Serving: Calories 160 (Calories from Fat 10); Fat 1g (Saturated 0g); Cholesterol 0mg; Sodium 840mg; Carbohydrate 37g (Dietary Fiber 11g); Protein 12g.

Navy Bean Soup

PREP: 1 hr 15 min; COOK: 1 hr 5 min

6 SERVINGS

If the soup seems a bit thick, just add a small amount of water and cook until desired consistency is reached.

1 package (16 ounces) dried navy beans, sorted and rinsed

8 cups water

1/2 cup chili sauce

1/2 teaspoon dried marjoram leaves

1 large onion, chopped (1 cup)

2 medium carrots, chopped (1 cup)

1 medium stalk celery, chopped (1/2 cup)

1 can (14 1/2 ounces) ready-to-serve vegetable broth

2 tablespoons chopped fresh parsley

1. Heat beans and water to boiling in 8-quart Dutch oven. Boil uncovered 2 minutes; remove from heat. Cover and let stand 1 hour.

2. Stir in remaining ingredients except parsley. Heat to boiling; reduce heat to low. Cover and simmer about 1 hour, stirring occasionally, until beans are tender.

3. Stir in parsley. Cook 2 to 3 minutes.

1 Serving: Calories 245 (Calories from Fat 10); Fat 1g (Saturated 0g); Cholesterol 0mg; Sodium 540mg; Carbohydrate 57g (Dietary Fiber 14g); Protein 16g.

Minestrone (page 14) and Lentil-Vegetable Soup

NAVY BEAN SOUP WITH HAM: *Add 1 cup diced fully cooked turkey ham with remaining ingredients in step 2. Continue as directed.*

Cuban Black Bean Soup

PREP: 1 hr 15 min; COOK: 2 hr 15 min

6 SERVINGS

Beans are a natural product harvested from fields, so even though the manufacturer has done it first, it's still important to sort through dried beans before cooking. Why? Because they often contain foreign matter such as small stones or shriveled and hard beans.

2 2/3 cups dried black beans (1 pound), sorted and rinsed

2 tablespoons vegetable oil

1 large onion, chopped (1 cup)

3 cloves garlic, finely chopped

3 cups vegetable or beef broth

3 cups water

1/4 cup dark rum or apple cider

1 1/2 teaspoons ground cumin

1 1/2 teaspoons dried oregano leaves

1 teaspoon liquid smoke, if desired

1 medium green bell pepper, chopped (1 cup)

1 large tomato, chopped (1 cup)

Chopped hard-cooked eggs, if desired

Chopped red onion, if desired

1. Place beans in 4-quart Dutch oven; add enough cold water to cover beans. Heat to boiling. Boil uncovered 2 minutes; remove from heat. Cover and let stand 1 hour. Drain and reserve beans.

2. Heat oil in same Dutch oven over medium heat. Cook 1 cup onion and the garlic in oil, stirring occasionally, until onion is tender.

3. Stir in remaining ingredients except tomato, eggs and red onion; heat to boiling; reduce heat to low. Cover and simmer about 2 hours, stirring occasionally, until beans are tender. Stir in tomato; simmer uncovered 10 minutes.

4. Serve soup topped with eggs and red onion.

1 Serving: Calories 315 (Calories from Fat 55); Fat 6g (Saturated 1g); Cholesterol 0mg; Sodium 500mg; Carbohydrate 62g (Dietary Fiber 16g); Protein 19g.

CUBAN BLACK BEAN SOUP WITH HAM:
Add 1 cup finely chopped fully cooked turkey ham with remaining ingredients in step 3. Continue as directed.

Southern Black-Eyed Pea Soup

PREP: **1 hr 10 min**; COOK: **1 hr 8 min**

6 SERVINGS

This hearty soup is similar to Hoppin' John, a favorite southern specialty typically made on New Year's Day to bring good luck for the coming year. Add a bit of spice by garnishing with a few drops of red pepper sauce but not so much to get you hoppin'!

1 package (16 ounces) dried black-eyed peas, sorted and rinsed

8 cups water

1/2 cup uncooked brown rice

2 teaspoons chopped garlic (from 4-ounce jar)

1/2 teaspoon dried marjoram leaves

2 medium stalks celery, chopped (1 cup)

2 medium carrots, chopped (1 cup)

1 medium onion, chopped (1/2 cup)

2 cans (14 1/2 ounces each) ready-to-serve vegetable broth

2 cups bite-size pieces spinach, collard greens or turnip greens

1. Heat peas and water to boiling in 8-quart Dutch oven. Boil uncovered 2 minutes; remove from heat. Cover and let stand 1 hour.

2. Stir in remaining ingredients except spinach. Heat to boiling; reduce heat to low. Cover and simmer 1 hour, stirring occasionally until peas are tender.

3. Stir in spinach. Cook 2 to 3 minutes.

1 Serving: Calories 280 (Calories from Fat 20); Fat 2g (Saturated 1g); Cholesterol 0mg; Sodium 630mg; Carbohydrate 62g (Dietary Fiber 16g); Protein 19g.

SOUTHERN BLACK-EYED PEA SOUP WITH HAM: *Add 2 cups diced turkey ham with the remaining ingredients in step 2. Continue as directed.*

Bean and Barley Soup

PREP: 8 min; COOK: 13 min

5 SERVINGS

1 tablespoon vegetable oil

2 small onions, cut in half and thinly sliced

2 cloves garlic, finely chopped

1 teaspoon ground cumin

1/2 cup uncooked quick-cooking barley

3 cups water

1/2 teaspoon salt

1 can (15 to 16 ounces) garbanzo beans, undrained

1 can (15 ounces) black beans, rinsed and drained

1 can (14 1/2 ounces) stewed tomatoes, undrained

1 package (10 ounces) frozen lima beans*

2 tablespoons chopped fresh cilantro or parsley

1. Heat oil in 4-quart Dutch oven over medium heat. Cook onions, garlic and cumin in oil, stirring occasionally, until onions are crisp-tender.

2. Stir in remaining ingredients except cilantro. Heat to boiling; reduce heat to low. Cover and simmer about 10 minutes or until lima beans are tender. Stir in cilantro.

*1 can (15 to 16 ounces) lima beans, rinsed and drained, can be substituted for the frozen lima beans.

1 Serving: Calories 380 (Calories from Fat 55); Fat 6g (Saturated 1g); Cholesterol 0mg; Sodium 890mg; Carbohydrate 79g (Dietary Fiber 18g); Protein 21g.

Vegetable Broth

PREP: 15 min; COOK: 1 hr 10 min

ABOUT 8 CUPS BROTH

Some strong vegetables, such as broccoli, cabbage, cauliflower, turnips and rutabagas, may be used sparingly with the mild vegetables. Use this broth in any recipe in this book calling for vegetable broth.

6 cups coarsely chopped mild vegetables (bell peppers, carrots, celery, leeks, mushroom stems, potatoes, spinach, zucchini)

1/2 cup parsley sprigs

8 cups cold water

2 tablespoons chopped fresh or 2 teaspoons dried basil leaves

2 tablespoons chopped fresh or 2 teaspoons dried thyme leaves

1 teaspoon salt

1/4 teaspoon cracked black pepper

1 medium onion, coarsely chopped (1/2 cup)

4 cloves garlic, chopped

2 bay leaves

1. Heat all ingredients to boiling in 4-quart Dutch oven; reduce heat to low. Cover and simmer 1 hour, stirring occasionally.

2. Cool broth slightly; strain broth. Cover and refrigerate up to 3 days or seal tightly and freeze up to 3 months. Stir before using.

1 Serving: Calories 5 (Calories from Fat 0); Fat 0g (Saturated 0g); Cholesterol 0mg; Sodium 290mg; Carbohydrate 1g (Dietary Fiber 0g); Protein 0g.

Roasted-Vegetable Broth

PREP: 15 min; BAKE: 1 hr; COOK: 1 hr 10 min

ABOUT **5** CUPS BROTH

Caramelizing turns vegetable starches into sugar, producing a rich, slightly sweet, roasted flavor. Caramelized vegetables will be deep golden brown and sticky to the touch. They also add extra depth of flavor to the broth.

6 cups large pieces mild vegetables (carrots, celery, whole mushrooms, potatoes and sweet potatoes)

2 medium onions, cut into fourths

2 cloves garlic, peeled

8 cups cold water

1/2 cup parsley sprigs

1 teaspoon salt

1/4 teaspoon cracked black pepper

1 sprig basil or 1 teaspoon dried basil leaves

1 sprig marjoram or 1 teaspoon dried marjoram leaves

1 sprig thyme or 1 teaspoon dried thyme leaves

1 bay leaf

1. Heat oven to 400°. Grease jelly roll pan, 15 1/2 × 10 1/2 × 1 inch. Spread vegetables, onions and garlic in pan. Bake uncovered 45 to 60 minutes or until vegetables are deep golden brown and tender.

2. Remove vegetables from pan; place in 4-quart Dutch oven. Pour 1/2 cup of the cold water in pan. Scrape pan to remove browned particles; add water and particles to vegetables.

3. Heat vegetables, remaining cold water and remaining ingredients to boiling; reduce heat to low. Cover and simmer 1 hour, stirring occasionally.

4. Cool broth slightly; strain broth. Cover and refrigerate up to 3 days or seal tightly and freeze up to 3 months. Stir before using.

1 Serving: Calories 10 (Calories from Fat 0); Fat 0g (Saturated 0g); Cholesterol 0mg; Sodium 450mg; Carbohydrate 2g (Dietary Fiber 0g); Protein 0g.

Jalapeño Potato Chowder

PREP: 15 min; COOK: 20 min

4 SERVINGS

Jalapeño chilies add a nice snappy flavor to this potato chowder, one that will satisfy even the most hearty appetites. Try serving with chunks of corn bread.

3 tablespoons margarine or butter

1 medium onion, chopped (1/2 cup)

1 small green bell pepper, chopped (1/2 cup)

3 tablespoons all-purpose flour

2 1/2 cups milk

3 cups diced cooked potatoes

1 cup fresh or frozen whole kernel corn

1 to 2 tablespoons fresh or canned chopped jalapeño chilies

3/4 teaspoon salt

1 teaspoon fresh or 1/4 teaspoon dried thyme leaves

1/2 cup shredded Swiss cheese (4 ounces), if desired

1. Melt margarine in 2-quart saucepan over medium heat. Cook onion and bell pepper in margarine 3 to 5 minutes, stirring occasionally, until crisp-tender.

2. Stir in flour. Gradually add milk, stirring constantly, until mixture is boiling.

3. Stir in remaining ingredients. Cook 5 to 10 minutes, stirring occasionally, until corn is tender. Serve soup topped with cheese.

1 Serving: Calories 310 (Calories from Fat 110); Fat 12g (Saturated 8g); Cholesterol 35mg; Sodium 600mg; Carbohydrate 46g (Dietary Fiber 4g); Protein 9g.

JALAPEÑO TUNA POTATO CHOWDER: *Omit whole kernel corn. Add 1 can (6 1/8 ounces) white tuna in water, drained, with remaining ingredients in step 3. Continue as directed.*

Chunky Vegetable Chowder

PREP: 12 min; COOK: 15 min

6 SERVINGS

When making the switch to meatless eating, you may find the transition easier if you cut your ingredients, as we have in this recipe, into larger pieces and chunks, which makes it seem plentiful and hearty. To reduce the fat and calories, use nonfat half-and-half.

1 tablespoon margarine or butter

1 medium green bell pepper, coarsely chopped (1 cup)

1 medium red bell pepper, coarsely chopped (1 cup)

7 medium green onions, sliced (3/4 cup)

3 cups water

3/4 pound new potatoes, cut into 1-inch pieces (2 1/2 cups)

1 tablespoon chopped fresh or 1 teaspoon dried thyme leaves

1/2 teaspoon salt

1 cup half-and-half

1/8 teaspoon pepper

2 cans (15 ounces each) cream-style corn

1. Melt margarine in 4-quart Dutch oven over medium heat. Cook bell peppers and onions in margarine 3 minutes, stirring occasionally.

2. Stir in water, potatoes, thyme and salt. Heat to boiling; reduce heat to low. Cover and simmer about 10 minutes or until potatoes are tender.

3. Stir in remaining ingredients; cook until hot (do not boil).

1 Serving: Calories 250 (Calories from Fat 70); Fat 8g (Saturated 4g); Cholesterol 15mg; Sodium 700mg; Carbohydrate 43g (Dietary Fiber 5g); Protein 6g.

Vegetable Chowder in Bread Bowls

PREP: 8 min; COOK: 10 min

4 SERVINGS

When serving soup in bread bowls, it helps to have the right utensils handy. For effortless eating, use a serrated steak knife, fork and spoon—this dish is a whole meal!

4 large hard rolls (about 3 1/2 inches in diameter)

2 cans (19 ounces each) ready-to-serve creamy potato soup with roasted garlic

1 package (16 ounces) frozen potatoes, sweet peas and carrots

1 can (15 to 16 ounces) kidney beans, rinsed and drained

1. Cut thin 2-inch-round slice from tops of rolls. Remove bread from inside of each roll, leaving 1/2-inch shell on side and bottom. (Reserve bread trimmings for another use.)

2. Heat soup, vegetables and beans in 3-quart saucepan over medium-high heat, stirring occasionally, 8 to 10 minutes until vegetables are tender and soup is hot.

3. Fill soup bowls one-third full with soup. Place rolls on top of soup. Spoon additional soup into rolls, allowing some soup to overflow into bowls.

1 Serving: Calories 515 (Calories from Fat 160); Fat 18g (Saturated 5g); Cholesterol 25mg; Sodium 1560mg; Carbohydrate 78g (Dietary Fiber 11g); Protein 21g.

SALMON VEGETABLE CHOWDER IN BREAD BOWLS: *Omit the kidney beans. Add 1 can (14 3/4 ounces) salmon, drained and flaked, with the vegetables in step 2. Continue as directed.*

Roasted-Vegetable Stew (page 38) and Vegetable Chowder in Bread Bowls

Legumes: Storage, Preparation and Cooking

SELECTION

Today it's easy to find a wide variety of legumes in your local supermarket. Legumes include beans, lentils, peas, soybeans and peanuts. More specialized legumes can be found in the health food section of large super-markets, in co-ops or in health food stores. You can also check specialty food mail-order catalogs if you are having a hard time finding an item locally. Often legumes are sold in bulk—load up, they store well, and once they are on hand, you'll be more likely to use them!

- When purchasing legumes, bright uniform color and smooth, unbroken seed coats indicate quality and freshness.

- Legumes of the same size will result in even cooking.

- Sort legumes before cooking to remove any damaged beans or foreign matter.

STORAGE

Dried Legumes

Most legumes can be stored indefinitely, but for optimum quality and flavor, a one- to two-year storage time is recommended.

- Store in original packaging or transfer to air-tight glass or plastic containers and label contents with starting storage date.

- Store in a cool (60°F or less), dry location.

Cooked Legumes

Refrigerator: Cooked legumes can be covered and stored in the refrigerator for two to three days.

Freezer: Cooked legumes can be frozen in airtight containers for up to eight months.

PREPARATION

Soaking legumes before cooking helps to hydrate them and shortens the cooking time. Follow one of the soaking methods below:

Soaking Legumes

Recent findings indicate that all legumes, except lentils, need to be boiled, uncovered, two minutes before cooking to destroy an enzyme that can cause some people to become ill. This boiling time eliminates the need for the traditional long-soaking method to help rehydrate legumes. Although eight- to twenty-four-hour soaking is not necessary, it does allow for more uniform swelling of legumes.

If you choose to soak legumes before cooking, use one of the following methods:

- **Long-Soak Method:** Place legumes in large saucepan or bowl in enough cold water to cover. Let stand at least eight hours or overnight. Drain and rinse. Boil beans two minutes in enough water to cover; drain.

- **Quick-Soak Method:** Boil beans two minutes in enough water to cover. Remove from heat; cover and let stand one hour before cooking; drain.

COOKING TIPS

Cooking legumes in a microwave oven is not recommended due to the amount of liquid necessary to hydrate them and the long, slow cooking time required. Use of a pressure-cooker is also not recommended due to the foam created when cooking legumes. The foam can clog the pressure valve and may cause a sudden release of pressure, which could force the lid off without warning.

- Beans of similar size can easily be interchanged in recipes.
- Dried legumes double or triple in volume as they cook, so be sure to use a sufficiently large pan or casserole.
- To prevent beans from foaming when cooking, add one tablespoon margarine or vegetable oil to the cooking water and cook as directed.
- Salt and acid tend to toughen beans. Add salt and acidic foods such as lemon juice, vinegar, tomatoes and tomato sauce, paste or juice only after the beans are soft, or the beans may not soften.
- High altitude and hard water may increase cooking times.
- Beans get drier with age and may take longer to cook. Very old beans may never soften completely.
- Simmer, rather than boil, beans and stir gently or the beans' skins may burst.

Legumes lose moisture with age, so you may find that you need more water than the recipe calls for. If all the water is absorbed but the legume isn't quite tender, add a little more water and cook longer. If it is tender but all the water hasn't been absorbed, drain if desired.

Legume Cooking Chart

Type of Bean (1 cup dried amount)	Amount of Water (using 3- to 4-quart saucepan)	Method of Cooking	Approximate Cooking Time	Approximate Yield in Cups
Adzuki	Enough to cover beans	Heat water and beans to a boil. Boil uncovered 2 minutes; reduce heat. Cover and simmer.	30 to 45 minutes	3
Anasazi, Black and Fava	Enough to cover beans	Heat water and beans to a boil. Boil uncovered 2 minutes; reduce heat. Cover and simmer.	1 to 2 hours	2
Black-Eyed Peas, Butter, Canellini and Pinto	Enough to cover beans	Heat water and beans to a boil. Boil uncovered 2 minutes; reduce heat. Cover and simmer.	1 to 1 1/2 hours	2 to 2 1/2
Garbanzo	Enough to cover beans	Heat water and beans to a boil. Boil uncovered 2 minutes; reduce heat. Cover and simmer.	2 to 2 1/2 hours	2
Great Northern	Enough to cover beans	Heat water and beans to a boil. Boil uncovered 2 minutes; reduce heat. Cover and simmer.	1 to 1 1/2 hours	2 to 3
Kidney	Enough to cover beans	Heat water and beans to a boil. Boil uncovered 2 minutes; reduce heat. Cover and simmer.	1 to 2 hours	2 to 2 1/2
Lentils	Enough to cover lentils	Heat water and lentils to a boil. Reduce heat. Cover and simmer.	30 to 45 minutes	2 to 2 1/4
Lima and Navy	Enough to cover beans	Heat water and beans to a boil. Boil uncovered 2 minutes; reduce heat. Cover and simmer.	1 to 1 1/2 hours	2

Type of Bean (1 cup dried amount)	Amount of Water (using 3- to 4-quart saucepan)	Method of Cooking	Approximate Cooking Time	Approximate Yield in Cups
Mung	Enough to cover beans	Heat water and beans to a boil. Boil uncovered 2 minutes; reduce heat. Cover and simmer.	45 to 60 minutes	2
Soy	Enough to cover beans	Heat water and beans to a boil. Boil uncovered 2 minutes; reduce heat. Cover and simmer.	3 to 4 hours	2
Split Peas	Enough to cover split peas	Heat water and beans to a boil. Boil uncovered 2 minutes; reduce heat. Cover and simmer.	45 to 60 minutes	2 1/4

Black Bean Vegetable Chowder

PREP: 8 min; COOK: 10 min

5 SERVINGS

2 tablespoons margarine or butter

1 large onion, chopped (1 cup)

3 tablespoons all-purpose flour

3/4 teaspoon ground cumin

1/2 teaspoon garlic salt

4 cups skim milk

1 package (16 ounces) frozen corn, broccoli and sweet red peppers

1 can (15 ounces) black beans, rinsed and drained

1 1/2 cups shredded sharp Cheddar or Monterey Jack cheese (6 ounces)

2 tablespoons chopped fresh cilantro or parsley

1. Melt margarine in 4-quart Dutch oven over medium heat. Cook onion in margarine, stirring occasionally, until crisp-tender.

2. Mix flour, cumin and garlic salt in medium bowl; gradually stir in milk with a wire whisk. Stir milk mixture into onion. Stir in vegetables and beans. Heat to boiling, stirring constantly. Boil and stir 1 minute; remove from heat.

3. Stir in 1 cup of the cheese until melted. Sprinkle each serving with remaining cheese and the cilantro.

1 Serving: Calories 430 (Calories from Fat 155); Fat 17g (Saturated 9g); Cholesterol 40mg; Sodium 850mg; Carbohydrate 52g (Dietary Fiber 8g); Protein 25g.

Three-Squash Stew

PREP: 15 min; COOK: 17 min

6 SERVINGS

Thick and hearty stews offer those with robust appetites something to sink their teeth into and this recipe fills the bill!

1 tablespoon olive or vegetable oil

1 large onion, sliced

1 clove garlic, finely chopped

1 jalapeño chili, seeded and finely chopped

2 medium zucchini, cut into 1/2-inch pieces (4 cups)

2 medium yellow summer squash, sliced (3 cups)

4 cups 1-inch pieces pattypan squash

1 pound green beans, cut into 1-inch pieces (3 cups)

1 cup fresh or frozen whole kernel corn

1 tablespoon chopped fresh or 1 teaspoon dried thyme leaves

2 cans (15 to 16 ounces each) kidney beans, undrained

1. Heat oil in 4-quart Dutch oven over medium heat. Cook onion, garlic and chili in oil about 2 minutes, stirring occasionally, until onion is tender.

2. Stir in remaining ingredients. Cook over low heat 10 to 15 minutes, stirring frequently, until squash is tender.

1 Serving: Calories 195 (Calories from Fat 25); Fat 3g (Saturated 1g); Cholesterol 0mg; Sodium 500mg; Carbohydrate 41g (Dietary Fiber 12g); Protein 13g.

Vegetable Gumbo Stew

PREP: 20 min; COOK: 15 min

4 SERVINGS

Cooking the flour and margarine until the color reaches a deep golden brown is the secret to the rich flavor in this gumbo.

1/4 cup margarine or butter

1/4 cup all-purpose flour

1 large onion, chopped (1 cup)

1 medium green bell pepper, chopped (1 cup)

2 cloves garlic, finely chopped

1 can (14 1/2 ounces) ready-to-serve vegetable broth

1/2 cup uncooked regular long grain rice

3/4 teaspoon dried thyme leaves

1/8 to 1/4 teaspoon ground red pepper (cayenne)

1 can (14 1/2 ounces) diced tomatoes, undrained

1 package (10 ounces) frozen cut okra, thawed and drained

1 package (10 ounces) frozen baby lima beans or black-eyed peas, thawed and drained

1. Melt margarine in 3-quart saucepan over medium-low heat. Stir in flour. Cook 10 to 12 minutes, stirring frequently, until deep golden brown. Stir in onion, bell pepper and garlic. Cook 2 to 3 minutes, stirring occasionally, until crisp-tender.

2. Gradually add broth, stirring constantly, until mixture thickens and boils. Stir in remaining ingredients except lima beans. Heat to boiling; reduce heat to medium-low. Cook 15 minutes, stirring occasionally.

3. Stir in lima beans. Cook 5 to 10 minutes, stirring occasionally, until lima beans are hot.

1 Serving: Calories 340 (Calories from Fat 115); Fat 13g (Saturated 8g); Cholesterol 30mg; Sodium 720mg; Carbohydrate 56g (Dietary Fiber 10g); Protein 10g.

Scandinavian Vegetable Stew

PREP: 10 min; COOK: 20 min

4 SERVINGS

Dill and hard-cooked egg add a Scandinavian touch to this soup brimming with fresh garden flavor. Always add dill weed close to the end of cooking as it loses flavor rather quickly when heated.

8 to 10 small red potatoes, cut into fourths (3 cups)

2 cups fresh or frozen baby-cut carrots

3 tablespoons margarine or butter

3 medium green onions, sliced (1/3 cup)

3 tablespoons all-purpose flour

2 cups milk

1/2 cup frozen green peas

3/4 teaspoon salt

1/8 teaspoon pepper

2 tablespoons chopped fresh or 1/2 teaspoon dried dill weed

1 hard-cooked egg, chopped

1. Mix potatoes and carrots in 3-quart saucepan; add enough water to cover. Heat to boiling; reduce heat to medium. Cover and cook 8 to 10 minutes or until tender; drain in colander. Wipe out saucepan with paper towel.

2. Melt margarine in same saucepan over medium heat. Cook onions in margarine 2 minutes, stirring occasionally. Stir in flour. Gradually add milk, stirring constantly, until mixture thickens and boils.

3. Stir in potatoes and carrots, peas, salt and pepper. Cook 5 to 6 minutes, stirring occasionally, until peas are tender.

4. Stir in dill weed. Cook 2 minutes, stirring constantly. Top each serving with chopped egg and, if desired, additional dill weed.

1 Serving: Calories 390 (Calories from Fat 115); Fat 13g (Saturated 8g); Cholesterol 85mg; Sodium 620mg; Carbohydrate 63g (Dietary Fiber 7g); Protein 12g.

SCANDINAVIAN VEGETABLE STEW WITH HAM: *Add 1 cup diced fully cooked turkey ham with peas in step 3. Continue as directed.*

Roasted-Vegetable Stew

PREP: 15 min; ROAST: 15 min; COOK: 20 min
6 SERVINGS

Loading up a soup or stew with vegetables and pasta makes it a very substantial meatless meal. Just add bread and a crisp salad and your meal is complete.

5 small red potatoes (3/4 pound), cut into fourths

1 large onion, cut into fourths

1 medium red bell pepper, cut into fourths and seeded

1 medium green bell pepper, cut into fourths and seeded

1 medium carrot, cut into 1/4-inch diagonal slices (1/2 cup)

1 small zucchini, cut into 1/2-inch slices

1/4 pound medium whole mushrooms

2 cloves garlic, finely chopped

2 tablespoons olive or vegetable oil

1 can (14 1/2 ounces) ready-to-serve vegetable or chicken broth

2 cans (14 1/2 ounces each) Italian-style stewed tomatoes, undrained

1 1/4 cups uncooked rotini pasta (4 ounces)

2 tablespoons chopped fresh parsley

Freshly ground pepper, if desired

1. Set oven control to broil. Toss potatoes, onion, bell peppers, carrot, zucchini, mushrooms, garlic and oil. Spread vegetable mixture, skin sides up, in ungreased jelly roll pan, 15 1/2 × 10 1/2 × 1 inch.

2. Broil with tops 4 to 6 inches from heat 10 to 15 minutes or until roasted. Remove vegetables as they become soft; cool. Remove skins from peppers. Coarsely chop potatoes, onion and peppers.

3. Mix vegetables, broth, tomatoes and pasta in 4-quart Dutch oven. Heat to boiling; reduce heat to low. Cover and simmer about 15 minutes, stirring occasionally, until pasta is tender. Sprinkle with parsley and pepper.

1 Serving: Calories 270 (Calories from Fat 45); Fat 5g (Saturated 1g); Cholesterol 0mg; Sodium 690mg; Carbohydrate 54g (Dietary Fiber 5g); Protein 7g.

Garden Patch Stew

PREP: 15 min; COOK: 40 min

6 SERVINGS

In a hurry? Substitute three cups frozen (unthawed) loose-pack mixed vegetables for the bell pepper, zucchini and yellow summer squash.

2 tablespoons margarine or butter

1 large onion, chopped (1 cup)

2 medium carrots, thinly sliced (1 cup)

2 cans (14 1/2 ounces each) ready-to-serve vegetable or chicken broth

3/4 cup uncooked brown or regular long grain white rice

4 new potatoes, cut into fourths

1 large red bell pepper, cut into 2 × 1/2-inch strips

1 medium zucchini, thinly sliced (1 cup)

1 medium yellow summer squash, thinly sliced (1 1/2 cups)

1 cup fresh or frozen whole kernel corn

1 tablespoon chopped fresh or 2 teaspoons dried basil leaves

1 teaspoon chopped fresh or 1/2 teaspoon dried thyme leaves

1/4 teaspoon pepper

1 can (15 to 16 ounces) garbanzo beans, rinsed and drained

1. Melt margarine in 4-quart Dutch oven over medium heat. Cook onion and carrots in margarine, stirring occasionally, until onions are tender.

2. Stir in broth and rice. Heat to boiling; reduce heat to low. Cover and simmer 20 minutes.

3. Stir in remaining ingredients. Cover and simmer 10 to 15 minutes or until vegetables are tender.

1 Serving: Calories 300 (Calories from Fat 55); Fat 6g (Saturated 2g); Cholesterol 0mg; Sodium 760mg; Carbohydrate 60g (Dietary Fiber 8g); Protein 10g.

The Bean Counter

Dried beans double or triple in volume as they cook, so be sure to use a large enough pan or casserole. When buying or cooking beans, use this chart as a guide:

This amount	Equals
8 ounces dried beans	1 cup uncooked
1 cup dried beans	2 to 3 cups cooked
1 pound dried beans	2 cups uncooked
2 cups dried beans	4 to 6 cups cooked
1 can (15 to 16 ounces) beans, drained	1 1/2 to 2 cups

Cajun Barley Stew

PREP: 10 min; COOK: 25 min

4 SERVINGS

Quick-cooking barley is a real time-saver! It cooks in about half the time that regular barely does. If Cajun or Creole seasoning isn't available, use 2 teaspoons chili powder, 1/2 teaspoon salt and 1/4 teaspoon pepper.

2 teaspoons vegetable oil

1 large onion, chopped (1 cup)

1 medium stalk celery, chopped (1/2 cup)

1/2 cup uncooked quick-cooking barley

5 cups tomato juice

1 to 2 teaspoons Cajun or Creole seasoning

2 cans (15 to 16 ounces each) great northern or navy beans, rinsed and drained

1/4 cup chopped fresh parsley

1. Heat oil in 12-inch skillet over medium-high heat. Cook onion and celery in oil, stirring occasionally, until crisp-tender.

2. Stir in remaining ingredients except parsley. Heat to boiling; reduce heat to low. Cover and simmer about 20 minutes or until barley is tender. Stir in parsley.

1 Serving: Calories 395 (Calories from Fat 35); Fat 4g (Saturated 1g); Cholesterol 0mg; Sodium 1570mg; Carbohydrate 84g (Dietary Fiber 18g); Protein 24g.

Barley Bean Stew

PREP: 10 min; COOK: 45 min

4 SERVINGS

1 tablespoon vegetable oil

1 large onion, chopped (1 cup)

1 can (14 1/2 ounces) ready-to-serve vegetable broth

1 can (14 1/2 ounces) diced tomatoes with basil, garlic and oregano, undrained

1/3 cup uncooked barley

1 cup frozen mixed vegetables

2 tablespoons ketchup

1 tablespoon Worcestershire sauce

1 can (15 to 16 ounces) great northern beans, rinsed and drained

2 tablespoons chopped fresh parsley

1. Heat oil in 3-quart saucepan over medium-high heat. Cook onion in oil 3 to 5 minutes, stirring occasionally, until crisp-tender.

2. Stir in broth, tomatoes and barley. Heat to boiling; reduce heat to medium. Cover and simmer 20 minutes, stirring occasionally.

3. Stir in remaining ingredients except parsley. Heat to boiling; reduce heat to medium. Cover and simmer 12 to 15 minutes, stirring occasionally, until barley is tender.

4. Stir in parsley. Cook 2 minutes. Sprinkle each serving with additional parsley if desired.

1 Serving: Calories 260 (Calories from Fat 35); Fat 4g (Saturated 1g); Cholesterol 0mg; Sodium 960mg; Carbohydrate 55g (Dietary Fiber 13g); Protein 14g.

Lentil and Vegetable Stew

PREP: 15 min; COOK: 47 min

5 SERVINGS

Try red lentils, they take less time to cook, and add a pretty color to the stew.

1 1/4 cups dried lentils (10 ounces), sorted and rinsed

3 cups water

2 medium potatoes, cut into 1-inch cubes (2 cups)

1 medium onion, chopped (1/2 cup)

1 medium stalk celery, chopped (1/2 cup)

2 cloves garlic, finely chopped

1 tablespoon chopped fresh parsley

4 teaspoons vegetable or beef bouillon granules

1 teaspoon ground cumin

2 medium zucchini, cut into 1/2-inch slices (4 cups)

Lemon wedges

1. Heat lentils and water to boiling in 4-quart Dutch oven; reduce heat to low. Cover and simmer about 30 minutes or until lentils are almost tender.

2. Stir in remaining ingredients except zucchini and lemon. Cover and simmer about 10 minutes or until potatoes are tender.

3. Stir in zucchini. Cover and simmer 5 to 7 minutes or until zucchini is crisp-tender. Serve stew with lemon wedges.

1 Serving: Calories 195 (Calories from Fat 10); Fat 1g (Saturated 0g); Cholesterol 0mg; Sodium 1250mg; Carbohydrate 44g (Dietary Fiber 13g); Protein 15g.

Eggplant and Black Bean Stew

PREP: 15 min; COOK: 25 min

4 SERVINGS

1 tablespoon olive or vegetable oil

1 large onion, chopped (1 cup)

1 medium green bell pepper, cut into 1-inch pieces

2 cups 1-inch pieces eggplant (3/4 pound)

1/2 cup water

1/4 teaspoon salt

1 medium zucchini, cut lengthwise in half, then cut crosswise into 1/4-inch slices (2 cups)

2 cans (14 1/2 ounces each) diced tomatoes with basil, garlic and oregano, undrained

1 can (15 ounces) black beans, rinsed and drained

Shredded Parmesan cheese, if desired

1. Heat oil in 3-quart saucepan over medium-high heat. Cook onion and bell pepper in oil 3 to 5 minutes, stirring occasionally, until crisp-tender.

2. Stir in remaining ingredients except cheese. Heat to boiling; reduce heat to medium-low. Cover and simmer 10 to 15 minutes, stirring occasionally, until vegetables are tender. Sprinkle each serving with cheese.

1 Serving: Calories 220 (Calories from Fat 45); Fat 5g (Saturated 1g); Cholesterol 0mg; Sodium 710mg; Carbohydrate 43g (Dietary Fiber 11g); Protein 12g.

Curried Sweet Potato and Lentil Stew

PREP: 10 min; COOK: 45 min

4 SERVINGS

Curry is made up of many flavors. The spices most often used to make aromatic curry powder include cardamom, chilies, cinnamon, fennel seed, fenugreek, cumin, turmeric, nutmeg, coriander and cloves. The apple juice added to this easy stew adds just a touch of sweetness and enhances its curry flavor.

2 tablespoons margarine or butter

1 large onion, chopped (1 cup)

1 tablespoon curry powder

2 tablespoons all-purpose flour

1 can (14 1/2 ounces) ready-to-serve vegetable broth

3/4 cup dried lentils (6 ounces), sorted and rinsed

1/2 teaspoon salt

1/2 cup apple juice

3 cups 1-inch pieces peeled sweet potatoes

1 cup frozen cut green beans

Sour cream or plain yogurt, if desired

Chutney, if desired

1. Melt margarine in 3-quart saucepan over medium-high heat. Cook onion and curry powder in margarine 2 minutes, stirring occasionally. Stir in flour; gradually add broth, stirring constantly, until thickened.

2. Stir in lentils and salt; reduce heat to low. Cover and simmer 20 minutes, stirring occasionally.

3. Stir in apple juice, sweet potatoes and green beans. Heat to boiling; reduce heat to low. Cover and simmer 15 to 20 minutes, stirring occasionally, until vegetables are tender. Top each serving with sour cream and chutney.

1 Serving: Calories 325 (Calories from Fat 65); Fat 7g (Saturated 2g); Cholesterol 0mg; Sodium 810mg; Carbohydrate 67g (Dietary Fiber 14g); Protein 13g.

Curried Sweet Potato and Lentil Stew

Home-Style Vegetable Chili

PREP: 15 min; COOK: 25 min

6 SERVINGS

Pasilla chilies are medium-hot in flavor and six to eight inches long. When fresh, they are sometimes referred to as chilaca chilies. Canned green chilies can be used if pasilla chilies are not available but the flavor might be slightly milder.

2 tablespoons vegetable oil

1 large onion, chopped (1 cup)

1 medium green bell pepper, chopped (1 cup)

2 medium carrots, chopped (1 cup)

1 pasilla chili, seeded and chopped (3/4 cup), or 1 can (4 ounces) diced green chilies

1 cup water

1 tablespoon chili powder

1 teaspoon ground cumin

3/4 teaspoon salt

2 cans (15 to 16 ounces each) red kidney beans, rinsed and drained

2 cans (14 1/2 ounces each) diced tomatoes, undrained

Shredded Cheddar cheese, if desired

1. Heat oil in 3-quart saucepan over medium-high heat. Cook onion, bell pepper, carrots and chili in oil 3 to 5 minutes, stirring occasionally until crisp-tender.

2. Stir in remaining ingredients except cheese. Heat to boiling; reduce heat to medium-low. Simmer uncovered 10 to 15 minutes, stirring occasionally, until vegetables are tender. Sprinkle each serving with cheese.

1 Serving: Calories 205 (Calories from Fat 55); Fat 6g (Saturated 1g); Cholesterol 0mg; Sodium 1010mg; Carbohydrate 36g (Dietary Fiber 9g); Protein 11g.

> HOME-STYLE TURKEY VEGETABLE CHILI: *Cook 1/2 pound ground turkey in oil until light brown before cooking vegetables and chili in step 1; drain if desired. Add vegetables and chili. Continue as directed.*

Chunky Vegetable Chili

PREP: 10 min; COOK: 24 min

4 SERVINGS

Beans go by so many names that it can be downright confusing! Garbanzo beans, also called chick-peas and ci-ci beans, are firm textured with a mild, nutty flavor.

2 medium potatoes, cut into 1-inch cubes (2 cups)

1 medium onion, chopped (1/2 cup)

1 medium bell pepper, coarsely chopped (1/2 cup)

1 tablespoon chili powder

1 teaspoon ground cumin

1 can (28 ounces) whole tomatoes, undrained

1 can (15 to 16 ounces) garbanzo beans, rinsed and drained

1 can (15 ounces) black beans, rinsed and drained

1 can (8 ounces) tomato sauce

1 medium zucchini, cut into 1-inch cubes (1 cup)

1. Mix all ingredients except zucchini in 4-quart Dutch oven. Heat to boiling, breaking up tomatoes; reduce heat to low. Cover and simmer 15 minutes, stirring occasionally.

2. Stir in zucchini. Cover and simmer 5 to 7 minutes, stirring occasionally, until zucchini is tender.

1 Serving: Calories 350 (Calories from Fat 35); Fat 4g (Saturated 1g); Cholesterol 0mg; Sodium 1090mg; Carbohydrate 75g (Dietary Fiber 16g); Protein 19g.

Ratatouille Chili

PREP: 10 min; COOK: 15 min

4 SERVINGS

From the Provence region of France, the popular dish of ratatouille is often served as a side dish or appetizer. The flavors typical of this dish include eggplant, zucchini, tomatoes, olive oil and garlic, all of which are found in this savory chili version.

2 tablespoons olive or vegetable oil

1 large eggplant (1 pound), cut into 1/2-inch cubes (4 cups)

1 large onion, chopped (1 cup)

1 medium green bell pepper, chopped (1 cup)

1 clove garlic, finely chopped

1/2 cup sliced zucchini

3 teaspoons chili powder

1 teaspoon chopped fresh or 1/4 teaspoon dried basil leaves

1/4 teaspoon salt

1 can (15 to 16 ounces) great northern beans, rinsed and drained

1 can (14 1/2 ounces) whole tomatoes, undrained

1 can (8 ounces) tomato sauce

1. Heat oil in 4-quart Dutch oven over medium-high heat. Cook eggplant, onion, bell pepper and garlic in oil, stirring occasionally, until vegetables are crisp-tender.

2. Stir in remaining ingredients, breaking up tomatoes. Cook about 10 minutes, stirring occasionally, until zucchini is tender.

1 Serving: Calories 265 (Calories from Fat 70); Fat 8g (Saturated 2g); Cholesterol 0mg; Sodium 900mg; Carbohydrate 48g (Dietary Fiber 13g); Protein 13g.

TURKEY RATATOUILLE CHILI: *Cook 1/2 pound ground turkey in oil until light brown before cooking vegetables in step 1; drain if desired. Add vegetables. Continue as directed.*

Cheesy Double-Bean Chili

PREP: 8 min; COOK: 20 min

6 SERVINGS

Chipotle chili powder adds a complex, deep, smoky flavor to this chili. Chipotle chili powder comes from ground chipotle chilies, which are dried, smoked jalapeño chilies.

2 tablespoons margarine or butter

1 medium onion, sliced

1 large clove garlic, finely chopped

1 can (28 ounces) whole tomatoes, undrained

1 can (15 to 16 ounces) kidney beans, rinsed and drained

1 can (15 to 16 ounces) pinto beans, rinsed and drained

1 can (4 ounces) chopped green chilies, drained

2 to 3 teaspoons chipotle chili powder or regular chili powder

1/2 cup shredded Cheddar cheese (2 ounces)

1 cup shredded Monterey Jack cheese (4 ounces)

1. Melt margarine in 3-quart saucepan over medium heat. Cook onion and garlic in margarine, stirring occasionally, until onion is tender.

2. Stir in remaining ingredients except cheeses, breaking up tomatoes. Heat to boiling; reduce heat to low. Cover and simmer 15 minutes, stirring occasionally.

3. Stir in Cheddar cheese and 1/2 cup of the Monterey Jack cheese. Heat over low heat, stirring occasionally, just until cheeses are melted. Sprinkle each serving with remaining Monterey Jack cheese.

1 Serving: Calories 295 (Calories from Fat 125); Fat 14g (Saturated 7g); Cholesterol 30mg; Sodium 1000mg; Carbohydrate 35g (Dietary Fiber 10g); Protein 17g.

CHEESY CHICKEN-BEAN CHILI: *Omit the kidney beans. Stir in 1 1/2 cups cut-up cooked chicken or turkey with remaining ingredients in step 2. Continue as directed.*

Three-Alarm Spaghetti and Pinto Bean Chili

PREP: 10 min; COOK: 25 min

4 SERVINGS

This chili recipe is based on the well-known Cincinnati chili, which is traditionally chili served over spaghetti. To save time and energy, the spaghetti is cooked right along with this spicy chili.

1 tablespoon vegetable oil

1 large onion, chopped (1 cup)

1 medium green bell pepper, chopped (1 cup)

3 cups water

1/2 cup taco sauce

2 teaspoons chili powder

1/2 teaspoon salt

1/4 teaspoon ground cinnamon

2 cans (10 ounces each) diced tomatoes and green chilies, undrained

4 ounces uncooked spaghetti, broken into thirds (1 1/2 cups)

1 can (15 to 16 ounces) pinto beans, rinsed and drained

Sour cream, if desired

Jalapeño chilies, if desired

1. Heat oil in 4-quart Dutch oven over medium-high heat. Cook onion and bell pepper in oil 3 to 5 minutes, stirring occasionally until crisp-tender.

2. Stir in remaining ingredients except spaghetti and beans. Heat to boiling; reduce heat to medium-low. Simmer uncovered 5 minutes, stirring occasionally.

3. Stir in spaghetti and beans. Heat to boiling; reduce heat to medium. Cook uncovered 8 to 10 minutes, stirring occasionally until spaghetti is tender. Garnish each serving with sour cream and jalapeño chilies.

1 Serving: Calories 315 (Calories from Fat 45); Fat 5g (Saturated 1g); Cholesterol 0mg; Sodium 1030mg; Carbohydrate 66g (Dietary Fiber 13g); Protein 14g.

Three-Alarm Spaghetti and Pinto Bean Chili

Red Beans and Rice Chili

PREP: 20 min; COOK: 25 min

4 SERVINGS

You'll enjoy this thick chili version of the famous Louisiana red beans and rice dish. Avocado adds a cool contrast to the spicy blast of the chili.

1 dried chipotle chili

1 tablespoon vegetable oil

1 large onion, chopped (1 cup)

1 can (14 1/2 ounces) ready-to-serve vegetable broth

1/2 cup uncooked regular long grain rice

1 cup fresh or frozen whole kernel corn

2 cans (14 1/2 ounces each) Mexican-style stewed tomatoes

1 can (15 to 16 ounces) light red kidney beans, rinsed and drained

Chopped or sliced avocado, if desired

1. Cover chili with very hot water. Let stand until chili is soft; drain. Seed and finely chop chili.

2. Heat oil in 2-quart saucepan over medium-high heat. Cook onion in oil 3 to 5 minutes, stirring occasionally, until onion is tender.

3. Stir in broth and rice. Heat to boiling; reduce heat to low. Cover and simmer 15 minutes, stirring occasionally.

4. Stir in chili and remaining ingredients except avocado. Heat to boiling; reduce heat to medium-low. Simmer uncovered 10 to 15 minutes, stirring frequently. Top each serving with avocado.

1 Serving: Calories 315 (Calories from Fat 45); Fat 5g (Saturated 1g); Cholesterol 0mg; Sodium 1370mg; Carbohydrate 64g (Dietary Fiber 8g); Protein 11g.

Three-Bean Chili

PREP: 10 min; COOK: 35 min

4 SERVINGS

1 can (14 1/2 ounces) ready-to-serve vegetable or chicken broth

1 large onion, chopped (1 cup)

2 cloves garlic, finely chopped

2 medium tomatoes, cut into 1/2-inch pieces (2 cups)

1 tablespoon chopped fresh or 1 teaspoon dried oregano leaves

2 1/2 teaspoons chili powder

1 can (15 to 16 ounces) chili beans in sauce, undrained

1 can (8 ounces) kidney beans, undrained

1 can (8 ounces) garbanzo beans, undrained

2 tablespoons chopped fresh cilantro or parsley

1. Heat 1/4 cup of the broth to boiling in 4-quart Dutch oven over medium heat. Cook onion and garlic in broth about 5 minutes, stirring occasionally, until onion is tender.

2. Stir in remaining broth and remaining ingredients except beans and cilantro. Heat to boiling; reduce heat to low. Cover and simmer 15 minutes, stirring occasionally.

3. Stir in beans. Heat to boiling; reduce heat to low. Simmer uncovered 10 minutes, stirring occasionally. Sprinkle with cilantro.

1 Serving: Calories 225 (Calories from Fat 25); Fat 3g (Saturated 1g); Cholesterol 0mg; Sodium 1160mg; Carbohydrate 46g (Dietary Fiber 11g); Protein 14g.

Pepper and Bean Chili with Salsa Cream

PREP: 5 min; COOK: 25 min

6 SERVINGS

Butter beans are really large, cream-colored lima beans. But that's where the similarity ends—butter beans don't taste like limas, they are very mild and rich. For a colorful chili, use three different colors of bell pepper—try green, red and yellow or orange bell pepper.

1 can (28 ounces) whole tomatoes,
   undrained

1 can (15 to 16 ounces) garbanzo beans,
   rinsed and drained

1 can (15 to 16 ounces) kidney beans, rinsed
   and drained

1 can (15 to 16 ounces) butter beans, rinsed
   and drained

1 can (15 ounces) tomato sauce

3 small bell peppers, cut into 1-inch pieces

1 Anaheim or jalapeño chili, seeded and
   chopped

1 to 2 tablespoons chili powder

1/4 teaspoon pepper

1/2 cup sour cream

3 tablespoons thick-and-chunky salsa

1. Mix all ingredients except sour cream and salsa in 4-quart Dutch oven. Heat to boiling, breaking up tomatoes; reduce heat to low. Cover and simmer 15 to 20 minutes, stirring occasionally, until bell peppers are tender.

2. Mix sour cream and salsa. Serve chili topped with salsa cream.

1 Serving: Calories 295 (Calories from Fat 65); Fat 7g (Saturated 3g); Cholesterol 15mg; Sodium 1190mg; Carbohydrate 55g (Dietary Fiber 14g); Protein 17g.

Three-Bean Enchilada Chili

PREP: 10 min; COOK: 25 min

5 SERVINGS

Pinto beans are two-tone kidney-shaped beans widely used in Central and South American cooking. They turn pink when cooked and are the most widely used bean in refried beans.

1 tablespoon vegetable oil

1 large onion, chopped (1 cup)

1 medium green bell pepper, chopped (1 cup)

1 can (28 ounces) crushed tomatoes, undrained

1 can (15 to 16 ounces) pinto beans, rinsed and drained

1 can (15 to 16 ounces) dark red kidney beans, rinsed and drained

1 can (15 ounces) black beans, rinsed and drained

1 can (10 ounces) enchilada sauce (1 1/4 cups)

1 teaspoon dried oregano leaves

Tortilla chips, broken, if desired

Shredded Cheddar cheese, if desired

1. Heat oil in 3-quart saucepan over medium-high heat. Cook onion and bell pepper in oil 5 minutes, stirring occasionally, until crisp-tender.

2. Stir in remaining ingredients except tortilla chips and cheese. Heat to boiling; reduce heat to medium-low. Simmer uncovered 10 to 15 minutes, stirring occasionally. Sprinkle each serving with chips and cheese.

1 Serving: Calories 315 (Calories from Fat 35); Fat 4g (Saturated 1g); Cholesterol 0mg; Sodium 1060mg; Carbohydrate 68g (Dietary Fiber 19g); Protein 21g.

TURKEY-BEAN ENCHILADA CHILI: *Cook 1/2 pound ground turkey in oil until light brown before cooking onion and bell pepper; drain if desired. Add onion and bell pepper. Continue as directed.*

Three-Bean Enchilada Chili

White Bean Chili

PREP: 10 min; COOK: 1 hr 10 min

6 SERVINGS

Hearty chilies are popular vegetarian dishes. White chili, a twist to traditional tomato-based chili, uses a vegetable or chicken broth as its base, rather than tomato.

1/4 cup margarine or butter

1 large onion, chopped (1 cup)

1 clove garlic, finely chopped

1/4 cup chopped fresh or 1 teaspoon dried basil leaves

3 cups vegetable or chicken broth

2 tablespoons chopped fresh cilantro or parsley

2 teaspoons chili powder

1/4 teaspoon ground cloves

2 cans (15 to 16 ounces each) great northern beans, undrained

1 medium tomato, chopped (3/4 cup)

Corn tortilla chips, if desired

1. Melt margarine in 4-quart Dutch oven over medium-high heat. Cook onion and garlic in margarine, stirring occasionally, until onion is tender. Stir in remaining ingredients except tomato and tortilla chips.

2. Heat to boiling; reduce heat to low. Cover and simmer 1 hour, stirring occasionally.

3. Serve chili topped with tomato and tortilla chips.

1 Serving: Calories 250 (Calories from Fat 70); Fat 8g (Saturated 2g); Cholesterol 0mg; Sodium 940mg; Carbohydrate 41g (Dietary Fiber 10g); Protein 14g.

CHICKEN AND WHITE BEAN CHILI: *Omit 1 can great northern beans. Increase vegetable broth to 3 1/2 cups. Stir in 3 cups cut-up cooked chicken with the remaining ingredients in step 1. Continue as directed.*

Ancho Black and White Bean Chili

PREP: 1 hr 15 min; COOK: 1 hr 5 min

4 SERVINGS

Ancho chilies are fairly mild but have a characteristic rich, slightly fruity flavor. When fresh, they are called poblano chilies. Serve this tasty chili with warm rolled flour tortillas.

1 1/4 cups dried black turtle beans
　　(8 ounces), sorted and rinsed

1 1/4 cups dried cannellini or great northern
　　beans (8 ounces), sorted and rinsed

8 cups water

1 cup thick-and-chunky salsa

1 teaspoon chopped garlic (from 4-ounce jar)

3/4 teaspoon salt

1 large onion, chopped (1 cup)

2 dried ancho chilies, seeded and chopped,
　　or 2 tablespoons canned diced green
　　chilies

1 can (14 1/2 ounces) diced tomatoes,
　　undrained

Sour cream, if desired

2 tablespoons chopped fresh cilantro

1. Heat beans and water to boiling in 8-quart Dutch oven. Boil uncovered 2 minutes; remove from heat. Cover and let stand 1 hour.

2. Stir in remaining ingredients except cilantro and sour cream. Heat to boiling; reduce heat to low. Cover and simmer 1 hour, stirring occasionally and adding water if necessary, until beans are tender.

3. Stir in cilantro. Top each serving with sour cream; sprinkle with additional chopped fresh cilantro if desired.

1 Serving: Calories 380 (Calories from Fat 20); Fat 2g (Saturated 1g); Cholesterol 0mg; Sodium 800mg; Carbohydrate 85g (Dietary Fiber 22g); Protein 28g.

2

Satisfying Sandwiches and Pizza

*Italian Broccoli and
Provolone Pizza (page 73)*

Italian Grinders

PREP: 12 min; COOK: 10 min

4 SANDWICHES

Can't resist the aroma and flavor of a meatball sandwich slathered in spaghetti sauce and adorned with peppers and onions? The solution is at hand. Frozen vegetable burgers mixed with just a few ingredients create memorable "meatless" meatballs.

4 frozen vegetable burgers, thawed

3 tablespoons grated Parmesan cheese

1 teaspoon Italian seasoning

4 teaspoons olive or vegetable oil

1 small onion, cut in half and sliced

1 small red bell pepper, cut into 1/4-inch strips

1 small green bell pepper, cut into 1/4-inch strips

4 hot dog buns, split

1/2 cup spaghetti sauce, heated

1. Mix burgers, cheese and Italian seasoning. Shape mixture into 16 balls. Heat 2 teaspoons of the oil in 10-inch nonstick skillet over medium heat. Cook burger balls in oil, turning frequently, until brown. Remove from skillet; keep warm.

2. Heat remaining 2 teaspoons oil in same skillet over medium heat. Cook onion and bell peppers in oil, stirring frequently, until crisp-tender.

3. Place 4 burger balls in each bun. Top with vegetable mixture. Serve with spaghetti sauce.

1 Sandwich: Calories 360 (Calories from Fat 115); Fat 13g (Saturated 4g); Cholesterol 5mg; Sodium 840mg; Carbohydrate 39g (Dietary Fiber 2g); Protein 24g.

Italian Vegetable Focaccia Sandwich

PREP: 5 min; BAKE: 30 min

4 SERVINGS

Focaccia bread is an Italian bread shaped into a large, flat round that's drizzled with olive oil and sometimes topped with Parmesan cheese or other items such as tomatoes or onions. It can be found in the bakery, deli and frozen-food sections of the grocery store.

1 round focaccia bread (10 to 12 inches in diameter), cut horizontally in half

1 1/2 cups shredded mozzarella or smoked provolone cheese (6 ounces)

1 package (16 ounces) frozen broccoli, cauliflower and carrots, thawed and drained

3 tablespoons fat-free Italian dressing

1. Heat oven to 400°.

2. Place bottom half of focaccia on ungreased cookie sheet. Sprinkle with 3/4 cup of the cheese. Spread vegetables over cheese; drizzle with dressing. Sprinkle with remaining 3/4 cup cheese. Replace top of focaccia.

3. Bake 12 to 15 minutes or until golden brown. Cut into wedges.

1 Serving: Calories 475 (Calories from Fat 160); Fat 18g (Saturated 7g); Cholesterol 25mg; Sodium 1290mg; Carbohydrate 61g (Dietary Fiber 5g); Protein 22g.

Italian Vegetable Focaccia Sandwich

Roasted Vegetable Wraps with Garlic Mayonnaise

PREP: 15 min; BAKE: 15 min

6 SANDWICHES

If you love garlic, but hate to chop it, consider keeping those handy little jars of chopped garlic on hand. If you like, use yellow summer squash instead of zucchini.

**1 medium bell pepper, cut into
  3/4-inch pieces**

**1 medium red onion, cut into
  1/2-inch wedges**

**1 medium zucchini, cut lengthwise in half,
  then cut crosswise into 1/4-inch slices**

1/4 pound mushrooms, cut into fourths

3 tablespoons olive or vegetable oil

1/2 teaspoon dried basil leaves

1/4 teaspoon salt

1/4 teaspoon coarsely ground pepper

Garlic Mayonnaise (right)

6 flour tortillas (8 or 10 inches in diameter)

1 1/2 cups shredded lettuce

1. Heat oven to 450°. Spread bell pepper, onion, zucchini and mushrooms in ungreased jelly roll pan, 15 1/2 × 10 1/2 × 1 inch.

2. Mix oil, basil, salt and pepper; brush over vegetables. Bake uncovered 12 to 15 minutes or until crisp-tender; cool slightly.

3. Spread about 2 teaspoons Garlic Mayonnaise down center of each tortilla to within 2 inches of bottom. Top with 1/6 of vegetable mixture, spreading to within 2 inches of bottom of tortilla. Top with 1/4 cup lettuce.

4. Fold one end of tortilla up about 1 inch over filling; fold right and left sides over folded end, overlapping. Fold remaining end down.

GARLIC MAYONNAISE

1/4 cup mayonnaise or salad dressing

1 tablespoon finely chopped fresh parsley

**1 teaspoon chopped garlic or 1/4 teaspoon
  garlic powder**

Mix all ingredients.

1 Sandwich: Calories 280 (Calories from Fat 155); Fat 17g (Saturated 3g); Cholesterol 5mg; Sodium 360mg; Carbohydrate 29g (Dietary Fiber 2g); Protein 5g.

GRILLED CHICKEN AND ROASTED VEGETABLE WRAPS WITH GARLIC MAYONNAISE: *Use 8 tortillas instead of 6. Thinly slice 2 warm or chilled grilled boneless, skinless chicken breast halves. Arrange the chicken on vegetables in step 3. Continue as directed.*

---

*Roasted Vegetable Wraps
with Garlic Mayonnaise*

Onion and Cheese Wedges

PREP: 5 min; COOK: 20 min;
BAKE: 20 min

6 SERVINGS

One-half cup crumbled feta or goat cheese (chèvre) can be substituted for the gorgonzola if desired.

2 tablespoons margarine or butter

2 medium onions, sliced

1 cup shredded mozzarella cheese (4 ounces)

1/2 cup finely crumbled gorgonzola or blue cheese (2 ounces)

1 round focaccia bread (10 to 12 inches in diameter), cut horizontally in half

1. Melt margarine in 10-inch skillet over medium-low heat. Cook onions in margarine 15 to 20 minutes, stirring occasionally, until onions are deep golden brown and tender; remove from heat.

2. Heat oven to 350°. Sprinkle half of the cheeses on bottom half of focaccia. Top with onions and remaining cheeses. Replace top of focaccia. Wrap tightly in aluminum foil.

3. Bake 15 to 20 minutes or until cheeses are melted. Cool 5 minutes. Cut into wedges.

1 Serving: Calories 355 (Calories from Fat 155); Fat 17g (Saturated 6g); Cholesterol 15mg; Sodium 900mg; Carbohydrate 40g (Dietary Fiber 2g); Protein 13g.

Pesto-Eggplant Sandwiches

PREP: 10 min; COOK: 10 min

4 OPEN-FACE SANDWICHES

The peak season for eggplant is generally August and September, but they usually are available all year. Choose eggplants that are firm and smooth skinned with no soft or wrinkled spots.

4 slices (1/2 inch thick) unpeeled eggplant

1 egg, beaten

1/3 cup seasoned dry bread crumbs

2 tablespoons olive or vegetable oil

4 thin slices red onion

4 slices (1 ounce each) provolone cheese

2 tablespoons pesto

4 slices (1/2 inch thick) Italian bread, toasted

8 thin slices cucumber

4 thin slices tomato

1. Dip eggplant slices into egg, then coat with bread crumbs. Heat oil in 10-inch skillet over medium heat. Cook eggplant in oil 3 to 4 minutes, turning once, until golden brown and crisp.

2. Top each eggplant slice with onion and cheese. Cover and cook 1 to 2 minutes or until cheese is melted.

3. Spread pesto on bread. Top with cucumber, tomato and eggplant.

1 Open-face Sandwich: Calories 275 (Calories from Fat 155); Fat 17g (Saturated 6g); Cholesterol 75mg; Sodium 450mg; Carbohydrate 23g (Dietary Fiber 3g); Protein 11g.

Toasted Colby–Jack Cheese Sandwiches

PREP: 10 min; COOK: 5 min

4 SANDWICHES

Colby–Monterey Jack cheese is also known as marble cheese or Co-Jack; it has a fairly mild flavor. For an all-American favorite, use process American cheese slices instead of Colby–Monterey Jack cheese.

8 slices pumpernickel bread

2 to 3 tablespoons creamy mustard-mayonnaise blend

1 medium avocado, thinly sliced

1 medium tomato, thinly sliced

4 slices (1 ounce each) Colby–Monterey Jack cheese

2 tablespoons margarine or butter

1. Spread each bread slice with mustard-mayonnaise spread. Top 4 slices with avocado, tomato and cheese. Top with remaining bread slices, spread side down.

2. Melt margarine in 12-inch skillet over medium heat. Cover and cook sandwiches in margarine 4 to 5 minutes, turning once, until both sides are crisp and cheese is melted.

1 Sandwich: Calories 355 (Calories from Fat 205); Fat 23g (Saturated 8g); Cholesterol 25mg; Sodium 600mg; Carbohydrate 32g (Dietary Fiber 6g); Protein 11g.

Super Grilled Cheese Sandwiches

PREP: 10 min; COOK: 8 min

4 SANDWICHES

Sourdough is a full-bodied bread, something you can really sink your teeth into, and that helps make you feel full and satisfied. Vary this hearty sandwich by using Cheddar, Muenster, Monterey Jack or provolone cheese.

1/2 pound thinly sliced Colby–Monterey Jack cheese

8 slices Italian sourdough, white or whole wheat bread

2 medium green onions, sliced (1/4 cup)

1 medium tomato, seeded and chopped (3/4 cup)

Nonstick cooking spray

1. Divide half of the cheese among 4 slices bread. Top with onions and tomato. Top with remaining cheese and bread. Spray cooking spray over each top slice of bread.

2. Place sandwiches, sprayed sides down, in skillet. Spray top slices of bread. Cook uncovered over medium heat about 5 minutes or until bottoms are golden brown. Turn and cook 2 to 3 minutes or until bottoms are golden brown and cheese is melted.

1 Sandwich: Calories 370 (Calories from Fat 190); Fat 21g (Saturated 143g); Cholesterol 60mg; Sodium 650mg; Carbohydrate 28g (Dietary Fiber 2g); Protein 19g.

Quesadillas

PREP: 10 min; BAKE: 5 min

6 SERVINGS

Here's a useful item to have on hand for quick meals: flour tortillas! These handy wrappers can be stuffed, rolled and folded for a super-easy meal. Look for regular, whole wheat, fat-free and flavored varieties.

2 cups shredded Cheddar or Monterey Jack cheese (8 ounces)

6 flour tortillas (8 to 10 inches in diameter)

1 small tomato, seeded and chopped (1/2 cup)

4 medium green onions, chopped (1/4 cup)

2 tablespoons canned chopped green chilies

Chopped fresh cilantro, if desired

1. Heat oven to 350°.

2. Sprinkle 1/3 cup of the cheese evenly over half of each tortilla. Sprinkle tomato, onions, chilies and cilantro over cheese. Fold tortillas over filling. Sprinkle with additional cilantro if desired. Place on ungreased cookie sheet.

3. Bake about 5 minutes or just until cheese is melted. Serve quesadillas whole, or cut each into 3 wedges, beginning cuts from center of folded sides.

1 Serving: Calories 290 (Calories from Fat 145); Fat 16g (Saturated 9g); Cholesterol 40mg; Sodium 440mg; Carbohydrate 26g (Dietary Fiber 2g); Protein 13g.

Eggwiches with Broccoli Sauce

PREP: 12 min; COOK: 15 min

4 SERVINGS

Eggs aren't just for breakfast! Busy weeknights and eggs just seem to go together because many egg dishes can be quick to prepare, as this one is. Toasted pine nuts or pumpkin seeds instead of sesame seed add extra zip.

1 1/2 cups chopped broccoli

1/2 cup chopped mushrooms (2 ounces)

2 tablespoons margarine or butter

1 tablespoon all-purpose flour

1/4 teaspoon salt

1 clove garlic, finely chopped

2/3 cup milk

1 egg yolk

4 slices whole wheat bread, toasted

4 eggs

2 teaspoons sesame seed, toasted*

1. Spray 10-inch skillet with cooking spray; heat over medium heat. Cook broccoli and mushrooms in skillet about 5 minutes, stirring occasionally, until broccoli is crisp-tender.

2. Melt margarine in 1-quart saucepan over low heat. Stir in flour, salt and garlic. Cook over low heat, stirring constantly, until mixture is smooth and bubbly; remove from heat. Mix milk and egg yolk until smooth; stir into flour mixture. Heat to boiling, stirring constantly. Boil and stir 1 minute. Stir in broccoli mixture; remove from heat.

3. Cut 2-inch hole in center of each slice toast. Spray same skillet with cooking spray; heat over medium heat. Place 1 slice toast in hot skillet; crack 1 egg into hole in toast. Cook until egg white and yolk are firm, not runny. Remove from skillet; keep warm.

4. Repeat with remaining toast and eggs. Top with broccoli mixture. Sprinkle with sesame seed. Serve immediately.

*To toast sesame seed, bake uncovered in ungreased shallow pan in 350° oven 8 to 10 minutes, stirring occasionally, until golden brown. Or cook in ungreased heavy skillet over medium heat about 2 minutes, stirring frequently until browning begins, then stirring constantly until golden brown.

1 Serving: Calories 255 (Calories from Fat 135); Fat 15g (Saturated 4g); Cholesterol 270mg; Sodium 460mg; Carbohydrate 20g (Dietary Fiber 3g); Protein 13g.

Dill and Dijon Egg-Salad Wraps

PREP: 10 min

5 SANDWICHES

Hard-cooked eggs can be made in advance and kept in the refrigerator for two days. If shell is hard to peel, hold egg in cold water while peeling.

4 hard-cooked eggs, chopped

2 tablespoons finely chopped red or green bell pepper

2 tablespoons finely chopped green onions

3 tablespoons mayonnaise or salad dressing

1 tablespoon Dijon mustard

1 tablespoon chopped fresh or 1/4 teaspoon dried dill weed

5 teaspoons mayonnaise or salad dressing

5 flour tortillas (6 or 8 inches in diameter)

1/2 cup shredded lettuce

1/2 cup alfalfa sprouts

1. Mix eggs, bell pepper, onions, 3 tablespoons mayonnaise, the mustard and dill weed.

2. Spread 1 teaspoon mayonnaise down center of each tortilla. Top with about 1/4 cup egg mixture, spreading to within 2 inches of bottom of tortilla. Top with lettuce and alfalfa sprouts.

3. Fold one end of tortilla up about 1 inch over filling; fold right and left sides over folded end, overlapping. Fold remaining end down.

1 Sandwich: Calories 285 (Calories from Fat 155); Fat 17g (Saturated 4g); Cholesterol 180mg; Sodium 370mg; Carbohydrate 25g (Dietary Fiber 1g); Protein 9g.

DILL AND DIJON CHICKEN-SALAD WRAPS: *Omit hard-cooked eggs. Add 1 cup chopped cooked chicken or turkey in step 1. Add 1 or 2 tablespoons mayonnaise for a moister mixture. Continue as directed.*

California Black Bean Burgers

PREP: 15 min; COOK: 15 min

5 SANDWICHES

Coating the patties with cornmeal gives them a delicious crispy coating. If the seasoned black beans aren't available, use unseasoned black beans and add one teaspoon chili powder.

1 can (15 ounces) black beans with cumin and chili spices, undrained

1 can (4 ounces) chopped green chilies, undrained

1 cup plain dry bread crumbs

1 egg, beaten

1/4 cup yellow cornmeal

2 tablespoons vegetable oil

5 hamburger buns, toasted

1 tablespoon mayonnaise or salad dressing

1 1/4 cups shredded lettuce

3 tablespoons thick-and-chunky salsa

1. Place beans in food processor or blender. Cover and process until slightly mashed; remove from food processor. Mix beans, chilies, bread crumbs and egg. Shape mixture into 5 patties, each about 1/2 inch thick. Coat each patty with cornmeal.

2. Heat oil in 10-inch skillet over medium heat. Cook patties in oil 10 to 15 minutes, turning once, until crisp and thoroughly cooked on both sides.

3. Spread bottom halves of buns with mayonnaise. Top with lettuce, patties, salsa and tops of buns.

1 Sandwich: Calories 385 (Calories from Fat 90); Fat 10g (Saturated 2g); Cholesterol 45mg; Sodium 940mg; Carbohydrate 67g (Dietary Fiber 9g); Protein 16g.

California Black Bean Burgers

Garbanzo Bean Sandwiches

PREP: 15 min

8 SERVINGS

Nuts and seeds are often incorporated into vegetarian diets, but it must be done with moderation as they can be high in fat. Fortunately, a little goes a long way in terms of flavor, and if nuts and seeds are lightly toasted, they become flavor giants!

1 can (15 to 16 ounces) garbanzo beans, rinsed and drained

1/2 cup water

2 tablespoons chopped fresh parsley

2 tablespoons chopped walnuts

1 tablespoon finely chopped onion

1 clove garlic, finely chopped

1/2 medium cucumber, sliced

4 whole wheat pita breads (6 inches in diameter)

Lettuce leaves

1 medium tomato, seeded and chopped (3/4 cup)

1/2 cup cucumber ranch dressing

1. Place beans, water, parsley, walnuts, onion and garlic in food processor or blender. Cover and process until smooth.

2. Cut cucumber slices into fourths. Cut each pita bread in half to form 2 pockets; line with lettuce leaves. Spoon 2 tablespoons bean spread into each pita half. Add tomato, cucumber and dressing.

1 Serving: Calories 230 (Calories from Fat 100); Fat 11g (Saturated 2g); Cholesterol 5mg; Sodium 360mg; Carbohydrate 30g (Dietary Fiber 4g); Protein 7g.

Meatless Meatball Pizza

PREP: 12 min; BAKE: 20 min

6 SERVINGS

You won't miss the sausage when you make "mini-meatballs" using Italian-flavored frozen vegetable burgers—it tastes just like Italian sausage pizza!

1 package (16 ounces) Italian bread shell or ready-to-serve pizza crust (12 to 14 inches in diameter)

2 frozen Italian-style vegetable burgers, thawed

3/4 cup pizza sauce

2 tablespoons sliced ripe olives

1 cup shredded mozzarella cheese (4 ounces)

1 cup shredded provolone cheese (4 ounces)

1. Heat oven to 425°.

2. Place bread shell on ungreased cookie sheet. Shape burgers into 1/2-inch balls. Spread pizza sauce over bread shell. Top with burger balls and olives. Sprinkle with cheeses.

3. Bake 18 to 20 minutes or until cheese is melted and light golden brown.

1 Serving: Calories 335 (Calories from Fat 135); Fat 15g (Saturated 7g); Cholesterol 25mg; Sodium 830mg; Carbohydrate 33g (Dietary Fiber 3g); Protein 20g.

What? No Big Juicy Hamburgers?

Chill out! There are many great-tasting vegetarian patties to replace the familiar hamburger. Eat them as a meal all by themselves or tucked into a bun with all the burger toppings you love. Most vegetarian burgers work well on the grill if they are marinated first, or brushed with a little vegetable oil to help prevent sticking. Vegetarian products that don't grill well are the low-fat or fat-free products because either they become rubbery or they crumble.

Legume Burgers

These burgers can be a combination of beans, lentils, vegetables, grains and tofu. Build a terrific burger by starting with California Black Bean Burgers (page 68), Butter Bean Patties with Southwestern Sauce (page 172) or Italian Bean Cakes (page 175).

Some examples of legume burgers in the freezer section of the supermarket are black beans with corn; multiple beans; brown rice with cheese; and lentil with brown rice and vegetables. Just follow the package directions to heat and eat.

Vegetable Burgers

Some patties are a combination of chopped vegetables with no added cheese, legumes, grains or tofu. Some combinations might be mushroom, carrot, ripe olive, onion and bell pepper. They are found in the freezer section of most supermarkets.

Cooked portobello mushroom or thick eggplant slices also make tasty "patties" on whole grain buns or bread. Jazz them up by topping with pesto cheese or fresh vegetables.

Meat Analog Burgers

Meat analog patties are nonmeat and often made from soy protein or tofu. Other ingredients include vegetables or grains. Some have beef, chicken, pork or fish flavors added, so they taste more like meat. You can find them in the freezer section of most supermarkets. Natural foods stores and food cooperatives usually carry a wide variety of these patties.

Sharp Cheddar, Artichoke and Red Onion Pizza

PREP: 5 min; BAKE: 10 min

4 SERVINGS

Artichoke hearts add a distinctive flavor to this easy pizza. Serve the pizza for a light supper, or cut into small squares for a great meatless appetizer. If roasted red bell peppers aren't available, use canned pimiento.

2 teaspoons margarine or butter

1 large red onion, sliced (2 cups)

1 package (16 ounces) Italian bread shell or ready-to-serve pizza crust (12 to 14 inches in diameter)

1/2 cup marinated artichoke hearts, drained and sliced

3 tablespoons sliced drained roasted red bell peppers (from 7-ounce jar)

1 cup shredded sharp Cheddar cheese (4 ounces)

1. Heat oven to 400°. Melt margarine in 8-inch skillet over medium heat. Cook onion in margarine 3 to 5 minutes, stirring occasionally, until crisp-tender.

2. Spread onion over bread shell. Top with artichoke hearts, bell peppers and cheese. Bake 8 to 10 minutes or until cheese is melted. Cut into wedges.

1 Serving: Calories 485 (Calories from Fat 200); Fat 22g (Saturated 9g); Cholesterol 35mg; Sodium 1190mg; Carbohydrate 60g (Dietary Fiber 4g); Protein 16g.

CHICKEN, ARTICHOKE AND RED ONION PIZZA: *Add 1 cup cubed cooked chicken or turkey with the artichoke hearts in step 2. Continue as directed.*

Italian Broccoli and Provolone Pizza

PREP: 10 min; BAKE: 20 min

6 SERVINGS

Provolone cheese has a slightly rich, smoky flavor that is delicious on this thin-crusted vegetable pizza. Shave off a few minutes of preparation time by purchasing sliced mushrooms.

2 cups frozen broccoli cuts

1 can (10 ounces) refrigerated pizza crust dough

1/2 cup Italian-style chunky tomato sauce

1 cup sliced mushrooms (3 ounces)

1/4 cup chopped drained roasted red bell peppers (from 7-ounce jar)

1 1/2 cups shredded provolone cheese (6 ounces)

1. Cook broccoli as directed on package until crisp-tender; drain.

2. Heat oven to 425°. Lightly grease jelly roll pan, 15 1/2 × 10 1/2 × 1 inch. Unroll pizza crust dough; press evenly in pan. Bake about 8 minutes or until light golden brown.

3. Spread tomato sauce over crust. Top with broccoli, mushrooms, bell peppers and cheese.

4. Bake 10 to 12 minutes or until crust is deep golden brown and cheese is melted. Cut into squares.

1 Serving: Calories 245 (Calories from Fat 100); Fat 11g (Saturated 5g); Cholesterol 25mg; Sodium 610mg; Carbohydrate 27g (Dietary Fiber 2g); Protein 11g.

Easy Broccoli Pizza

PREP: 8 min; COOK: 7 min; BAKE: 10 min

4 SERVINGS

Get inspired to eat more vegetables; check out pre-washed, precut, bagged produce—ready right now!

1 package (16 ounces) Italian bread shell or ready-to-serve pizza crust (12 to 14 inches in diameter)

2/3 cup pizza sauce

1 teaspoon olive or vegetable oil

1 clove garlic, finely chopped

1 small onion, finely chopped (1/4 cup)

2 cups broccoli slaw

2/3 cup shredded mozzarella cheese

2 tablespoons grated Parmesan cheese

1. Heat oven to 450°.

2. Place bread shell on ungreased cookie sheet. Spread pizza sauce evenly over bread shell.

3. Heat oil in 8-inch skillet over medium heat. Cook garlic and onion in oil, stirring occasionally, until onion is tender. Stir in broccoli slaw. Cook 5 to 6 minutes, stirring occasionally and adding up to 2 tablespoons water if necessary to prevent sticking, until broccoli is crisp-tender.

4. Spoon vegetable mixture evenly over pizza sauce. Sprinkle with cheeses.

5. Bake about 10 minutes or until cheese is melted.

1 Serving: Calories 345 (Calories from Fat 110); Fat 12g (Saturated 4g); Cholesterol 10mg; Sodium 690mg; Carbohydrate 49g (Dietary Fiber 4g); Protein 14g.

Cheesy Tomato and Bell Pepper Pizzas

PREP: 12 min; BAKE: 12 min

6 SERVINGS

For individual pizzas, use six pita breads, about six inches in diameter, for the Italian shells. Keep prebaked pizza crusts on hand for impromptu meals and snacks—you can top them a thousand ways to satisfy even the pickiest eaters.

3 packages (8 ounces each) Italian bread shells or 6 pita breads (6 inches in diameter)

6 ounces reduced-fat cream cheese (Neufchâtel) or regular cream cheese, softened (from 8-ounce package)

6 tablespoons pesto

4 roma (plum) tomatoes, sliced

3/4 cup 1/2-inch pieces yellow bell pepper

2 medium green onions, sliced (1/4 cup)

1 tablespoon chopped fresh or 1/2 teaspoon dried basil leaves

1 cup shredded mozzarella cheese (4 ounces)

2 tablespoons freshly grated Parmesan cheese

1. Heat oven to 450°.

2. Place bread shells on ungreased large cookie sheet. Spread cream cheese on bread shells to within 1/4 inch of edges. Gently spread pesto over cream cheese. Top with tomatoes, bell pepper and onions. Sprinkle with basil and cheeses.

3. Bake 7 to 12 minutes or until cheeses are melted.

1 Serving: Calories 545 (Calories from Fat 245); Fat 27g (Saturated 9g); Cholesterol 30mg; Sodium 1330mg; Carbohydrate 61g (Dietary Fiber 3g); Protein 18g.

Sun-Dried Tomato and Herb Pizza

PREP: 10 min; BAKE: 10 min

6 SERVINGS

If you have your own herb garden, add your own oregano and basil, or substitute some other herbs that you like, such as marjoram, rosemary, savory or thyme.

1 package (16 ounces) Italian bread shell or ready-to-serve pizza crust (12 to 14 inches in diameter)

1/4 cup soft cream cheese with chives and onions

1/2 cup oil-packed sun-dried tomatoes, drained and sliced

2 tablespoons chopped fresh oregano leaves

2 tablespoons chopped fresh basil leaves

1 cup shredded mozzarella cheese (4 ounces)

1/4 cup shredded Cheddar cheese (1 ounce)

1. Heat oven to 425°. Place bread shell on ungreased cookie sheet. Spread with cream cheese. Top with tomatoes, oregano and basil. Sprinkle with mozzarella and Cheddar cheeses.

2. Bake 8 to 10 minutes or until cheese is melted. Cut into wedges.

1 Serving: Calories 285 (Calories from Fat 115); Fat 13g (Saturated 6g); Cholesterol 25mg; Sodium 440mg; Carbohydrate 32g (Dietary Fiber 1g); Protein 11g.

Pizza Monterey

PREP: 14 min; BAKE: 25 min

6 SERVINGS

Refrigerated pizza dough and frozen vegetables let you make this pizza very quickly! If the vegetable mixture we've listed doesn't excite your taste buds, go ahead and use the combination you love—the recipe will work just fine.

1 can (10 ounces) refrigerated pizza crust dough

2 cups shredded reduced-fat Monterey Jack cheese (8 ounces)

1 package (16 ounces) frozen broccoli, cauliflower and carrots, thawed and drained

1/2 cup reduced-fat ranch dressing

1. Heat oven to 425°. Lightly grease 12-inch pizza pan or rectangular pan, 13 × 9 × 2 inches.

2. Unroll pizza crust dough; press evenly in pan. Bake about 10 minutes or until light golden brown.

3. Sprinkle 1 cup of the cheese over crust. Cut large pieces of vegetables into bite-size pieces if necessary. Spread vegetables over cheese. Drizzle with dressing. Sprinkle with remaining 1 cup cheese.

4. Bake 12 to 15 minutes or until crust is deep golden brown and cheese is melted.

1 Serving: Calories 290 (Calories from Fat 115); Fat 13g (Saturated 5g); Cholesterol 20mg; Sodium 630mg; Carbohydrate 29g (Dietary Fiber 2g); Protein 16g.

Niçoise French Bread Pizza

PREP: 15 min; BAKE: 25 min

4 SERVINGS

Salade Niçoise *is a salad from the French city of Nice, perched on the glamorous French Riviera. The salad is often served with crusty French bread so a French bread pizza is a perfect adaptation. For do-ahead convenience, bake the vegetables and refrigerate them up to two days before preparing the pizza.*

4 roma (plum) tomatoes, cut into 1/4-inch slices

1 medium green bell pepper, cut into 1/4-inch rings

1 large onion, thinly sliced

1/2 cup Italian dressing

1/2 loaf (1-pound size) French bread, cut horizontally in half

2 hard-cooked eggs, sliced

1/4 cup sliced ripe olives

1 cup finely shredded mozzarella cheese (4 ounces)

1. Heat oven to 450°. Line jelly roll pan, 15 1/2 × 10 1/2 × 1 inch, with aluminum foil. Spread tomatoes, bell pepper and onion on foil. Brush both sides of vegetables with about half of the dressing. Bake uncovered 12 to 15 minutes or until onion is crisp-tender.

2. Reduce oven temperature to 375°. Remove vegetables and foil from pan. Place bread halves, cut sides up, in pan. Brush with remaining dressing. Top evenly with roasted vegetables, eggs, olives and cheese.

3. Bake 8 to 10 minutes or until cheese is melted. Cut into 2-inch slices.

1 Serving: Calories 320 (Calories from Fat 145); Fat 16g (Saturated 5g); Cholesterol 85mg; Sodium 620mg; Carbohydrate 34g (Dietary Fiber 3g); Protein 13g.

> NIÇOISE TUNA FRENCH BREAD PIZZA:
> *Add 1 can (6 ounces) white tuna in water, drained, with the roasted vegetables in step 2. Continue as directed.*

Niçoise French Bread Pizza

Thai Vegetable Pizza

PREP: 9 min; BAKE: 20 min

6 SERVINGS

Purchased peanut sauce, found in the ethnic-foods section of your grocery store, can be used in place of the peanut butter spread, soy sauce, vinegar and sugar. Use a scant one cup of purchased sauce.

6 fat-free flour tortillas (8 to 10 inches in diameter)

2/3 cup reduced-fat peanut butter spread

1/4 cup soy sauce

2 tablespoons seasoned rice vinegar

2 teaspoons sugar

2 cups shredded mozzarella cheese (8 ounces)

2 cups fresh bean sprouts

1 package (16 ounces) frozen stir-fry vegetables, thawed and drained

1. Heat oven to 400°. Place tortillas on ungreased cookie sheet. Bake 5 minutes.

2. Mix peanut butter spread, soy sauce, vinegar and sugar; spread over tortillas. Top each with 1/4 cup cheese. Spread bean sprouts and stir-fry vegetables evenly over tortillas. Sprinkle with remaining 1/2 cup cheese.

3. Bake 10 to 15 minutes or until cheese is melted.

1 Serving: Calories 415 (Calories from Fat 155); Fat 17g (Saturated 6g); Cholesterol 20mg; Sodium 1410mg; Carbohydrate 20g (Dietary Fiber 3g); Protein 23g.

> THAI CHICKEN PIZZA: *Omit bean sprouts. Add 2 cups chopped chicken with the stir-fry vegetables in step 2. Continue as directed.*

Santa Fe Nacho Pizzas

PREP: 15 min; BAKE: 25 min

5 SERVINGS

These individual pizzas are great for a snack or light lunch, and the recipe doubles easily.

1 can (10.8 ounces) refrigerated dough for large flaky biscuits

3 tablespoons black bean dip

1/3 cup thick-and-chunky salsa

2 tablespoons chopped canned green chilies

2 medium green onions, chopped (2 tablespoons)

2 tablespoons sliced ripe olives

3/4 cup shredded Monterey Jack and Cheddar marble cheese (3 ounces)

1 tablespoon chopped fresh cilantro

1. Heat oven to 350°. Unroll biscuit dough. Press or roll dough into 5-inch circles on ungreased cookie sheet. Spread dough with bean dip. Top with salsa, chilies, onions and olives. Sprinkle with cheese and cilantro.

2. Bake 20 to 25 minutes or until crust is deep golden brown and cheese is melted.

1 Serving: Calories 185 (Calories from Fat 100); Fat 11g (Saturated 5g); Cholesterol 20mg; Sodium 570mg; Carbohydrate 16g (Dietary Fiber 1g); Protein 6g.

> SANTA FE CHICKEN NACHO PIZZAS: *Sprinkle 1 cup chopped cooked chicken or turkey over the bean dip in step 1. Continue as directed.*

Santa Fe Nacho Pizzas

Pizza Mexicana

PREP: 10 min; BAKE: 10 min

6 SERVINGS

Jicama adds a refreshing crunch along with vitamin C and potassium to this tasty pizza.

6 pita breads (6 inches in diameter)

1 can (15 ounces) tomato sauce with tomato bits

2 cups shredded peeled jicama

1 can (4 ounces) chopped green chilies, drained

1 1/2 cups shredded taco-flavored cheese (6 ounces)

1. Heat oven to 350°. Place pita breads on ungreased cookie sheet. Spread tomato sauce over pita breads. Top with jicama and chilies. Sprinkle with cheese.

2. Bake 8 to 10 minutes or until cheese is melted.

1 Serving: Calories 295 (Calories from Fat 80); Fat 9g (Saturated 6g); Cholesterol 30mg; Sodium 1120mg; Carbohydrate 45g (Dietary Fiber 5g); Protein 13g.

CHICKEN PIZZA MEXICANA: *Omit jicama. Add 2 cups shredded cooked chicken with the chilies in step 1. Continue as directed.*

Mediterranean Pizza

PREP: 12 min; BAKE: 10 min

6 SERVINGS

1 package (16 ounces) Italian bread shell or ready-to-serve pizza crust (12 to 14 inches in diameter)

1 1/2 cups shredded mozzarella cheese (6 ounces)

1 jar (7 ounces) roasted red bell peppers, drained and diced (3/4 cup)

1 jar (7 ounces) sun-dried tomatoes in oil, drained and chopped

2 roma (plum) tomatoes, sliced

1 small red onion, sliced

2 pepperoncini peppers (bottled Italian peppers), drained and sliced

2 tablespoons sliced pimiento-stuffed olives

2 tablespoons sliced ripe olives

1 tablespoon chopped fresh or 1 teaspoon dried basil leaves

1. Heat oven to 450°. Place bread shell on ungreased cookie sheet. Sprinkle with 1 cup of the cheese. Top with remaining ingredients except basil. Sprinkle with remaining 1/2 cup cheese and the basil.

2. Bake about 10 minutes or until cheese is melted.

1 Serving: Calories 300 (Calories from Fat 110); Fat 12g (Saturated 5g); Cholesterol 15mg; Sodium 580mg; Carbohydrate 38g (Dietary Fiber 3g); Protein 13g.

MEDITERRANEAN SHRIMP PIZZA: *Add 1 can (4 1/2 ounces) medium shrimp, drained and rinsed, with the remaining ingredients in step 1. Continue as directed.*

Layered Pizza Pie

PREP: 10 min; BAKE: 40 min

6 SERVINGS

Eat your spinach! Mom was right, spinach is very good for you. It's rich in iron and also contains calcium, vitamin A and vitamin C. And it's rich in taste appeal, especially in this pie, which will satisfy even the pickiest eaters.

2 cans (10 ounces each) refrigerated pizza crust dough

1 can (8 ounces) pizza sauce (1 cup)

1 jar (4 1/2 ounces) sliced mushrooms, drained

1/4 cup sliced ripe olives

1 1/2 cups shredded mozzarella cheese (6 ounces)

2 packages (10 ounces each) frozen chopped spinach, thawed and squeezed to drain

1 teaspoon olive or vegetable oil

1 tablespoon grated Parmesan cheese

1. Heat oven to 400°. Lightly grease pie plate, 9 × 1 1/4 inches.

2. Unroll 1 can of pizza crust dough. Place dough in pie plate; press against bottom and side of pie plate to form crust.

3. Mix pizza sauce and mushrooms; spoon onto dough. Layer with olives, 3/4 cup of the mozzarella cheese, the spinach and remaining 3/4 cup mozzarella cheese.

4. Unroll remaining can of dough. Press dough into 9-inch circle; place over filling. Pinch edges of dough together to seal; roll up edge of dough or flute to form rim. Cut several slits in dough. Brush with oil; sprinkle with Parmesan cheese.

5. Bake 35 to 40 minutes or until deep golden brown.

1 Serving: Calories 445 (Calories from Fat 135); Fat 15g (Saturated 5g); Cholesterol 15mg; Sodium 1000mg; Carbohydrate 63g (Dietary Fiber 5g); Protein 19g

LAYERED ITALIAN SAUSAGE PIZZA PIE: *Cook 1/2 pound bulk Italian turkey sausage until done. Add sausage with olives in step 3. Continue as directed.*

3

Meal-Sized Salads

Spring Vegetable Paella
(page 84)

Spring Vegetable Paella

PREP: 15 min; COOK: 15 min

6 SERVINGS

It's not generally well-known, but green peas are a good source of fiber and they also rank as one of the top three favorite vegetables in the United States. Saffron is a fragrant spice that is the dried stigmas of crocus and gives food a pretty yellow color. Because it is expensive, you may prefer to use ground turmeric as an affordable substitute.

1 pound asparagus, cut into 2-inch pieces

3 cups broccoli flowerets

2 teaspoons olive or vegetable oil

1 medium red bell pepper, chopped (1 cup)

2 small zucchini, chopped (1 1/4 cups)

1 medium onion, chopped (1/2 cup)

3/4 teaspoon salt

1/2 teaspoon saffron threads or 1/4 teaspoon ground turmeric

4 cups cooked brown or white rice, cold

2 large tomatoes, seeded and chopped (2 cups)

2 cans (15 to 16 ounces each) garbanzo beans, rinsed and drained

1 package (10 ounces) frozen green peas, thawed and drained

1. Heat 1 inch water to boiling in 2-quart saucepan. Add asparagus and broccoli. Heat to boiling; boil about 4 minutes or until crisp-tender; drain.

2. Heat oil in 10-inch skillet over medium-high heat. Cook asparagus, broccoli, bell pepper, zucchini, onion, salt and saffron in oil about 5 minutes, stirring occasionally, until onion is crisp-tender.

3. Stir in remaining ingredients. Serve on platter or individual serving plates lined with lettuce.

1 Serving: Calories 405 (Calories from Fat 65); Fat 7g (Saturated 1g); Cholesterol 0mg; Sodium 650mg; Carbohydrate 79g (Dietary Fiber 14g); Protein 20g.

SPRING VEGETABLE AND CHICKEN PAELLA: *Omit 1 can of garbanzo beans. Add 1 1/2 cups chopped cooked chicken or turkey with remaining ingredients in step 3. Continue as directed.*

Broiled Portobello Mushroom Salad

PREP: 10 min; BROIL: 7 min

4 SERVINGS

During the summer, cook the portobello mushrooms on an outdoor grill for extra flavor. If goat cheese isn't your favorite, use 1/2 cup whipped herbed or plain cream cheese instead.

3/4 pound sliced portobello mushrooms

1/2 cup fat-free Italian dressing

4 cups bite-size pieces mixed salad greens

1/2 cup crumbled herbed or plain chèvre (goat) cheese (2 ounces)

1/2 cup shredded mozzarella cheese (2 ounces)

4 slices bread, toasted and cut in half

4 roma (plum) tomatoes, sliced

1. Set oven control to broil. Spray broiler pan rack with cooking spray. Brush dressing on both sides of mushrooms; reserve remaining dressing. Place mushrooms on rack in broiler pan. Broil with tops 2 to 4 inches from heat 4 minutes; turn. Broil about 3 minutes longer or just until mushrooms are tender.

2. While mushrooms are broiling, divide salad greens among 4 plates. Mix cheeses; spread on toast.

3. Place mushrooms on salad greens. Top with tomatoes. Drizzle with remaining dressing. Serve with toast.

1 Serving: Calories 220 (Calories from Fat 80); Fat 9g (Saturated 5g); Cholesterol 25mg; Sodium 570mg; Carbohydrate 26g (Dietary Fiber 3g); Protein 12g.

Autumn Harvest Salad

PREP: 20 min; BROIL: 8 min
4 SERVINGS

Peeling the squash is easier if it is first microwaved whole on high power for three minutes. Red cabbage, a cruciferous vegetable, contains a good amount of vitamin C and some vitamin A.

1 small butternut squash (1 pound)

2 firm ripe pears

1 tablespoon margarine or butter, melted

3 cups finely chopped red cabbage

1 small Granny Smith apple, chopped

1/4 cup chopped walnuts, toasted (page 18)

1/2 cup raspberry or regular vinaigrette dressing

1. Set oven control to broil. Spray broiler pan rack with cooking spray. Peel squash. Cut squash crosswise into 1/2-inch slices; remove seeds. Cut pears lengthwise into 8 pieces; cut out cores. Brush squash and pears with margarine. Place squash on rack in broiler pan.

2. Broil with tops 2 to 3 inches from heat 4 minutes; turn. Add pears, cut sides up, to rack. Broil 3 to 4 minutes or until squash and pears are tender.

3. Place cabbage on large platter. Top with squash and pears. Sprinkle with apple and walnuts. Drizzle with dressing.

1 Serving: Calories 290 (Calories from Fat 180); Fat 20g (Saturated 3g); Cholesterol 5mg; Sodium 280mg; Carbohydrate 29g (Dietary Fiber 5g); Protein 3g.

Garden Vegetable Salad

PREP: 20 min
4 SERVINGS

Salad olives are a great buy all the way around. Not only do they cost less than whole olives, but they eliminate the need for chopping or slicing. Reduced-fat buttermilk dressing, instead of peppercorn ranch, is also delicious on this vegetable-packed salad.

3 cups bite-size pieces cauliflower (1 pound)

2 cups bite-size pieces broccoli (5 ounces)

1 cup cherry tomatoes, cut in half

3/4 cup diced Colby cheese (4 ounces)

1/2 cup sliced celery (1 medium stalk)

1/4 cup pimiento-stuffed salad olives

1/2 cup reduced-fat peppercorn ranch dressing

1. Mix all ingredients except dressing in large bowl.

2. Add dressing; toss until vegetables are evenly coated with dressing.

1 Serving: Calories 200 (Calories from Fat 135); Fat 15g (Saturated 6g); Cholesterol 20mg; Sodium 520mg; Carbohydrate 11g (Dietary Fiber 3g); Protein 8g.

> GARDEN VEGETABLE TUNA SALAD: *Add 1 can (6 ounces) tuna in water, drained, with all ingredients in step 1. Continue as directed.*

Autumn Harvest Salad

Caramelized-Vegetable Salad

PREP: 10 min; COOK: 20 min

6 SERVINGS

Balsamic vinegar is a great flavor booster; you may want to try it in place of the more familiar cider vinegar. Balsamic vinegar is a dark, brown-colored vinegar with a rich, mellow, smooth and slightly sweet flavor.

2 pounds small red potatoes, cut into 1-inch pieces

1 pound green beans, cut in half

1/2 teaspoon salt

1/3 cup margarine or butter

2 large onions, chopped (2 cups)

1/4 cup balsamic or cider vinegar

1/4 cup packed brown sugar

1/4 teaspoon salt

6 cups bite-size pieces leaf lettuce

Freshly ground pepper, if desired

1. Heat 1 inch water to boiling in 4-quart Dutch oven. Add potatoes, green beans and 1/2 teaspoon salt. Heat to boiling; reduce heat to medium. Cover and cook about 10 minutes or until vegetables are tender; drain and set aside.

2. While vegetables are cooking, melt margarine in 12-inch skillet over medium-high heat. Cook onions in margarine 10 to 12 minutes, stirring occasionally, until golden brown. Stir in vinegar, brown sugar and 1/4 teaspoon salt. Pour onion mixture over potatoes and green beans; stir until coated.

3. Line large platter with lettuce. Top with warm vegetables. Sprinkle with pepper.

1 Serving: Calories 285 (Calories from Fat 90); Fat 10g (Saturated 3g); Cholesterol 0mg; Sodium 430mg; Carbohydrate 50g (Dietary Fiber 6g); Protein 5g.

> CARAMELIZED-VEGETABLE SALAD WITH SALMON: *Add 1 can (14 3/4 ounces) salmon, drained and flaked, on top of warm vegetables in step 3. Continue as directed.*

Caramelized-Vegetable Salad

Winter Cottage Fruit Salad

PREP: 15 min

4 SERVINGS

For a cool and quick salad or snack, keep canned fruits in the refrigerator. Canned fruits make this the ideal winter salad, but you can also use fresh peaches and pears when they are in season.

12 Boston or Bibb lettuce leaves

1 can (15 to 16 ounces) sliced peaches, chilled and drained

1 can (15 to 16 ounces) sliced pears, chilled and drained

1 cup fresh or frozen raspberries

1 container (16 ounces) reduced-fat small curd cottage cheese

1/2 package (8-ounce size) reduced-fat cream cheese (Neufchâtel), softened

1/4 cup maraschino cherry juice

1/4 cup chopped pecans

1. Divide lettuce among 4 plates. Top with peaches, pears and raspberries. Add 1/2-cup scoop cottage cheese in center of each salad.

2. Mix cream cheese and cherry juice until smooth; drizzle over salads. Sprinkle with pecans.

1 Serving: Calories 310 (Calories from Fat 110); Fat 12g (Saturated 5g); Cholesterol 25mg; Sodium 600mg; Carbohydrate 36g (Dietary Fiber 5g); Protein 20g.

*Winter Cottage
Fruit Salad*

Egg-Asparagus Salad

Prep: 15 min; **Cook:** 5 min

4 SERVINGS

How do you get hard-cooked eggs without a green ring around the yolk? Place raw eggs in saucepan and add enough cold water just to cover eggs. Heat to boiling. Remove the saucepan from the heat. Cover the saucepan and let the eggs stand in the water eighteen minutes. Immediately drain and rinse with cold water; peel.

Dijon Vinaigrette (right)

2 teaspoons vegetable oil

1 pound asparagus, cut into 2-inch pieces

1 medium red bell pepper, cut into 1-inch pieces

1 package (4 ounces) mixed baby greens

4 hard-cooked eggs, chopped

1 cup croutons

1. Prepare Dijon Vinaigrette.

2. Heat oil in 10-inch nonstick skillet over medium-high heat. Cook asparagus and bell pepper in oil about 5 minutes, stirring frequently, until crisp-tender.

3. Line large platter with baby greens. Top with asparagus and bell pepper. Sprinkle with eggs and croutons. Drizzle with vinaigrette.

DIJON VINAIGRETTE

3 tablespoons vegetable oil

2 tablespoons red wine vinegar

1 1/2 teaspoons sugar

1 1/2 teaspoons Dijon mustard

1/2 teaspoon salt

1/8 teaspoon pepper

Shake all ingredients in tightly covered container.

1 Serving: Calories 240 (Calories from Fat 160); Fat 18g (Saturated 4g); Cholesterol 215mg; Sodium 440mg; Carbohydrate 13g (Dietary Fiber 2g); Protein 9g.

> **EGG-ASPARAGUS SALAD WITH SHRIMP:** *Arrange 1/2 pound cooked, peeled and deveined shrimp on the egg in step 3. Continue as directed.*

Greek Pasta Salad

PREP: 15 min; CHILL: 1 hr

5 SERVINGS

Feta cheese is bursting with sharp, tangy, salty flavor. This crumbly cheese is traditionally made from goat's or sheep's milk, but due to its popularity, is often made with cow's milk. Crumbled blue cheese, in place of the feta, is also good on this salad.

1 1/4 cups uncooked rosamarina (orzo) pasta (8 ounces)

2 cups thinly sliced cucumber

1/2 cup chopped red onion

1/2 cup Italian dressing

1 medium tomato, chopped (3/4 cup)

1 can (15 to 16 ounces) garbanzo beans, rinsed and drained

1 can (2 1/4 ounces) sliced ripe olives, drained

1/2 cup crumbled feta cheese (2 ounces)

1. Cook and drain pasta as directed on package. Rinse with cold water; drain.

2. Mix pasta and remaining ingredients except cheese in large glass or plastic bowl.

3. Cover and refrigerate at least 1 hour to blend flavors but no longer than 24 hours. Top with cheese.

1 Serving: Calories 370 (Calories from Fat 145); Fat 16g (Saturated 4g); Cholesterol 15mg; Sodium 610mg; Carbohydrate 49g (Dietary Fiber 5g); Protein 12g.

Pasta Cancún

PREP: 5 min; COOK: 23 min

4 SERVINGS

Citrus peel can be shredded whenever it's convenient and then frozen for up to six months for use at any time. Cumin isn't in your spice rack? Use 1/4 teaspoon dried oregano leaves instead.

4 cups uncooked radiatore (nugget) pasta (12 ounces)

2 cans (14 1/2 ounces each) Southwestern-style diced tomatoes with chili spices, undrained

1 can (15 ounces) black beans, rinsed and drained

1 teaspoon finely shredded lime peel

1/2 teaspoon ground cumin

1/2 medium bell pepper, cut into 2 × 1/4-inch strips

1/4 cup sour cream

4 lime wedges

Cilantro sprigs, if desired

1. Cook and drain pasta as directed on package.

2. Heat tomatoes to boiling in same pan. Stir in pasta, beans, lime peel, cumin and bell pepper; reduce heat. Simmer 2 to 3 minutes, stirring occasionally, until warm.

3. Top each serving with sour cream and lime wedges; garnish with cilantro. Squeeze juice from lime wedges over pasta mixture.

1 Serving: Calories 610 (Calories from Fat 55); Fat 6g (Saturated 3g); Cholesterol 10mg; Sodium 820mg; Carbohydrate 141g (Dietary Fiber 13g); Protein 27g.

Sweet-and-Sour Oriental Pasta Salad

COOK: 20 min; PREP: 10 min

6 SERVINGS

Cashews are the nut of the cashew apple. Their high fat content gives them their delicious buttery flavor. Because of that fat, cashews should be stored in the refrigerator or freezer so they don't become rancid.

3 ounces uncooked capellini (angel hair) pasta, broken in half

4 cups shredded Chinese (napa) cabbage

1 cup sliced mushrooms (3 ounces)

1 cup Chinese pea pods, cut in half (4 ounces)

1 can (8 ounces) sliced water chestnuts, drained

3/4 cup sweet-and-sour sauce

1/3 cup plain yogurt

1/2 cup chopped salted cashews

1. Cook and drain pasta as directed on package. Rinse with cold water; drain.

2. Place pasta, cabbage, mushrooms, pea pods and water chestnuts in large bowl. Mix sweet-and-sour sauce and yogurt with fork. Pour over salad; toss until coated. Sprinkle with cashews.

1 Serving: Calories 195 (Calories from Fat 55); Fat 6g (Saturated 2g); Cholesterol 0mg; Sodium 210mg; Carbohydrate 32g (Dietary Fiber 3g); Protein 6g.

SWEET-AND-SOUR ORIENTAL PASTA-SHRIMP SALAD: *Add 1 pound cooked peeled deveined medium shrimp with pasta, and add 1/2 teaspoon salt with yogurt in step 2. Continue as directed.*

---

*Sweet-and-Sour
Oriental Pasta Salad*

Marinated Artichokes, Peppers and Pasta

PREP: 10 min; COOK: 15 min

4 SERVINGS

A last-minute meal is always possible if you keep pasta and a variety of bottled and canned vegetables and sauces on hand. A medium red or green bell pepper, chopped, can be used instead of the roasted red bell peppers. For a crunchy change, try two tablespoons chopped almonds or walnuts for the pine nuts.

2 2/3 cups uncooked penne pasta (8 ounces)

1 jar (7 ounces) roasted red bell peppers, drained and chopped

1 jar (6 to 7 ounces) marinated artichoke hearts, undrained

1 jar (2.5 ounces) sliced mushrooms, drained

3 tablespoons torn fresh basil leaves

2 tablespoons shredded Asiago or Parmesan cheese

1/2 teaspoon pepper

2 tablespoons pine nuts

1. Cook and drain pasta as directed on package.

2. While pasta is cooking, mix remaining ingredients except nuts in large bowl. Add pasta; toss. Sprinkle with nuts.

1 Serving: Calories 280 (Calories from Fat 45); Fat 5g (Saturated 2g); Cholesterol 2mg; Sodium 230mg; Carbohydrate 53g (Dietary Fiber 5g); Protein 11g.

Spinach Pasta Salad

PREP: 20 min; COOK: 15 min

6 SERVINGS

3 cups uncooked farfalle (bow-tie) pasta (6 ounces)

1 small tomato, cut into fourths

1/2 cup pesto

1/4 teaspoon salt

1/4 teaspoon pepper

4 cups bite-size pieces spinach leaves

2 medium carrots, thinly sliced (1 cup)

1 small red onion, thinly sliced

1 can (14 ounces) quartered artichokes hearts, rinsed and drained

1. Cook and drain pasta as directed on package. Rinse with cold water; drain.

2. While pasta is cooking, place tomato, pesto, salt and pepper in food processor or blender. Cover and process 30 seconds.

3. Toss pasta, pesto mixture and remaining ingredients.

1 Serving: Calories 385 (Calories from Fat 110); Fat 12g (Saturated 3g); Cholesterol 5mg; Sodium 460mg; Carbohydrate 63g (Dietary Fiber 7g); Protein 13g.

Spinach Pasta Salad

MARINATED ARTICHOKES, PEPPERS, CHICKEN AND PASTA: *Add 1 1/2 cups cubed cooked chicken or turkey with the remaining ingredients in step 2. Continue as directed.*

The Neighborhood Co-op Store

Call them cooperatives, natural foods stores or whole foods stores, but no matter what you call them one thing is for certain: these stores are fun, interesting and informative! If your vision of a co-op store is a throwback to the 1960s, unorganized and a little too laid-back, you're mistaken. These types of food stores are a great boon to a variety of people with a variety of needs. Not only do the stores serve the vegetarian community, but they also cater to people with special diets, allergies, health problems, environmental concerns, a preference for organic foods, the desire to buy in bulk and the need to buy foods that can be purchased in very small quantities. Memberships are offered at many stores, giving you a discount on your purchases, but you do not need to be a member to shop at these stores.

Just take a look at a sampling of what your friendly neighborhood co-op is likely to offer:

- Full line of groceries, including produce, canned goods, refrigerated, frozen, delis, toiletries and household cleaning products. Vegetarian pet foods and cosmetics not tested on animals or containing all natural ingredients can be found, too!

- Bulk grains, pastas, flours, beans, legumes, dried fruits, herbs, spices, teas, oils, syrups and many other ingredients.

- Specialty foods to meet many dietary needs, including vegetarianism and allergies (egg-free, wheat-free, gluten-free, yeast-free, lactose-free, salt-free and sugar-free, to name a few).

- Nutritional supplements, natural remedies, wellness and medicinal remedies and ingredients, homeopathic products and pharmaceutical products.

- Natural and environmentally friendly household cleaning and lawn-care products.

- Information pamphlets, magazines, newsletters and classes that address food, ingredients, health, environment, gardening and a wide variety of other subjects.

Warm Salsa Pasta Salad

PREP: 5 min; COOK: 15 min

4 SERVINGS

Dried pasta made from wheat is a good source of complex carbohydrates, and egg-free pasta is free of fat and cholesterol. If you like, use small or medium pasta shells instead of the elbow macaroni.

1 package (7 ounces) elbow macaroni (2 cups)

1 cup frozen whole kernel corn

1 cup salsa

1 small green bell pepper, chopped (1/2 cup)

1 can (14 1/2 ounces) no-salt-added whole tomatoes, undrained

1 can (15 to 16 ounces) kidney beans, rinsed and drained

Freshly ground pepper, if desired

1. Cook and drain macaroni as directed on package.

2. While macaroni is cooking, heat remaining ingredients except beans and pepper to boiling in 2-quart saucepan over medium heat, breaking up tomatoes; reduce heat. Simmer uncovered 5 minutes.

3. Stir in macaroni and beans; cook until hot. Serve with pepper.

1 Serving: Calories 315 (Calories from Fat 20); Fat 2g (Saturated 1g); Cholesterol 0mg; Sodium 500mg; Carbohydrate 69g (Dietary Fiber 10g); Protein 15g.

Couscous-Vegetable Salad

PREP: 11 min; COOK: 7 min

6 SERVINGS

Couscous is on the most-wanted list because it's versatile, tastes great and is so fast to prepare—just five minutes! This tiniest form of pasta is granular semolina and it's the staple of North African cuisine.

1 cup uncooked couscous

Olive oil-flavored or regular nonstick cooking spray

1 medium zucchini, cut into 1/4-inch slices (2 cups)

1 medium yellow summer squash, cut into 1/4-inch slices (1 1/2 cups)

1 large red bell pepper, cut into 1-inch pieces

1/2 medium red onion, cut into 8 wedges

1 container (7 ounces) refrigerated pesto with sun-dried tomatoes or regular pesto

2 tablespoons balsamic or cider vinegar

1. Prepare couscous as directed on package.

2. Spray 10-inch nonstick skillet with cooking spray; heat over medium-high heat. Add zucchini, yellow squash, bell pepper and onion; spray lightly with cooking spray. Cook vegetables about 5 minutes, stirring frequently, until crisp-tender.

3. Toss couscous, vegetable mixture, pesto and vinegar in large bowl. Serve warm or cool.

1 Serving: Calories 290 (Calories from Fat 155); Fat 17g (Saturated 4g); Cholesterol 5mg; Sodium 270mg; Carbohydrate 30g (Dietary Fiber 3g); Protein 7g.

Couscous-Stuffed Avocados

PREP: 15 min; COOK: 5 min

4 SERVINGS

Preparing couscous in fruit juice adds a distinctive flavor in this slightly sweet salad. To save time, use one can (eleven ounces) mandarin oranges, drained, for the fresh oranges.

1 cup orange juice

3/4 cup uncooked couscous

1 medium carrot, shredded (3/4 cup)

2 medium green onions, sliced (1/4 cup)

2 avocados, peeled and sliced

2 medium oranges, peeled and sectioned

1/4 cup French dressing

2 tablespoons salted sunflower nuts

1. Heat orange juice to boiling in 1-quart saucepan; remove from heat. Stir in couscous. Cover and let stand 5 minutes. Stir in carrot and onions.

2. Divide couscous among 4 plates. Arrange avocado slices and orange sections around couscous.

3. Drizzle salads with dressing. Sprinkle with nuts.

1 Serving: Calories 395 (Calories from Fat 190); Fat 21g (Saturated 3g); Cholesterol 1mg; Sodium 180mg; Carbohydrate 52g (Dietary Fiber 10g); Protein 9g.

Dilled Gouda and Barley Salad

PREP: 15 min

4 SERVINGS

Cook it now, eat it later! Cooked barley can be covered and stored in the refrigerator for up to one week.

1/3 cup sun-dried tomatoes (not oil-packed)

2 cups cold cooked barley

3/4 cup shredded smoked Gouda cheese (3 ounces)

1/3 cup reduced-fat mayonnaise or salad dressing

2 teaspoons chopped fresh or 3/4 teaspoon dried dill weed

1 teaspoon lemon juice

1/4 teaspoon salt

1 small zucchini, coarsely chopped (1 cup)

Red leaf lettuce

1. Cover tomatoes with enough hot water to cover. Let stand 5 minutes; drain and chop.

2. Mix tomatoes and remaining ingredients except lettuce. Serve on lettuce.

1 Serving: Calories 240 (Calories from Fat 115); Fat 13g (Saturated 5g); Cholesterol 25mg; Sodium 640mg; Carbohydrate 27g (Dietary Fiber 5g); Protein 9g.

DILLED GOUDA AND CHICKEN SALAD:
Omit the barley. Add 2 cups cubed cooked chicken or turkey with remaining ingredients in step 2. Continue as directed.

Three-Bean and Barley Salad

PREP: 5 min; CHILL: 1 hr

4 SERVINGS

Canned three-bean salad comes with its own built-in salad dressing, which makes it a convenient little gem to have on hand. To keep up the convenience theme, use quick-cooking barley for this recipe.

1 can (15 ounces) three-bean salad, undrained

1 1/2 cups cooked barley

2 medium tomatoes, chopped (1 1/2 cups)

3 cups bite-size pieces salad greens

2 tablespoons sunflower nuts

1. Mix three-bean salad, barley and tomatoes in bowl. Cover and refrigerate about 1 hour or until chilled.

2. Spoon bean mixture onto salad greens. Sprinkle with nuts.

1 Serving: Calories 160 (Calories from Fat 25); Fat 3g (Saturated 0g); Cholesterol 0mg; Sodium 480mg; Carbohydrate 34g (Dietary Fiber 7g); Protein 6g.

Mexican Stuffed Tomatoes

PREP: 20 min

4 SERVINGS

If you are avoiding dairy products, check your co-op or health food store for soymilk products such as cheese and yogurt. Cold cooked white rice or barley can be used instead of the brown rice.

4 medium tomatoes

2 cups cold cooked brown rice

1/2 cup shredded Cheddar cheese (2 ounces)

1/4 cup sour cream

1/4 cup salsa

2 teaspoons lime or lemon juice

1/2 teaspoon salt

2 medium green onions, sliced (1/4 cup)

Shredded iceberg lettuce

1. Cut 1/2-inch slice from top of each tomato. Scoop out tomato pulp and seeds. Discard seeds, and chop pulp.

2. Mix tomato pulp and remaining ingredients except lettuce. Spoon mixture into tomato shells. Serve on lettuce.

1 Serving: Calories 220 (Calories from Fat 80); Fat 9g (Saturated 5g); Cholesterol 25mg; Sodium 450mg; Carbohydrate 31g (Dietary Fiber 4g); Protein 8g.

Southwestern Wild Rice Salad in Bread Bowls

PREP: 15 min

4 SERVINGS

All rice is not the same! Because brown rice still has the germ and bran layer, it takes longer to cook, about forty-five to fifty minutes versus twenty minutes for regular long grain white rice, but it's worth the time. Cook a double batch, and keep rice in the freezer for nights you want brown rice in a snap. Use chili powder if cumin isn't available.

1 cup cooked wild rice

1 cup cooked brown or white rice

3 tablespoons chopped fresh cilantro

1 can (15 to 16 ounces) pinto beans, rinsed and drained

1 can (11 ounces) whole kernel corn with red and green peppers, drained

1 can (4 ounces) chopped green chilies, drained

3 tablespoons white wine vinegar

1 tablespoon Dijon mustard

1/4 teaspoon ground cumin

1/4 teaspoon pepper

4 large Kaiser rolls (about 3 1/2 inches in diameter)

1/2 cup shredded part-skim mozzarella cheese (2 ounces)

1. Mix wild rice, brown rice, cilantro, beans, corn and chilies in medium bowl. Mix vinegar, mustard, cumin and pepper; toss with rice mixture.

2. Cut 1/2-inch-thick slice from tops of rolls. Remove bread from inside of each roll, leaving 1/2-inch shell on side and bottom. Reserve bread trimmings for another use.

3. Spoon rice mixture into rolls. Sprinkle with cheese.

1 Serving: Calories 485 (Calories from Fat 65); Fat 7g (Saturated 3g); Cholesterol 10mg; Sodium 1190mg; Carbohydrate 95g (Dietary Fiber 13g); Protein 23g.

SOUTHWESTERN CHICKEN-WILD RICE SALAD IN BREAD BOWLS: *Omit pinto beans. Add 1 1/2 cups cubed cooked chicken or turkey with wild rice in step 1. Continue as directed.*

Fruited Rice Salad with Toasted Almonds

PREP: 20 min

4 SERVINGS

One-third cup honey Dijon or poppy seed dressing may be substituted for the orange marmalade, soy sauce and ginger. Don't have time to peel fresh oranges? Use 1 can (11 ounces) mandarin orange segments, drained, instead.

3 tablespoons orange marmalade

1 tablespoon soy sauce

1/4 teaspoon ground ginger

3 cups cold cooked white rice

1 cup seedless red grapes

2 medium oranges, peeled and chopped

2 small kiwifruit, peeled and sliced

Lettuce leaves

1/3 cup slivered almonds, toasted (page 18)

1. Mix marmalade, soy sauce and ginger in large bowl.

2. Add remaining ingredients except lettuce and almonds; toss. Serve on lettuce; sprinkle with almonds.

1 Serving: Calories 325 (Calories from Fat 55); Fat 6g (Saturated 1g); Cholesterol 0mg; Sodium 270mg; Carbohydrate 66g (Dietary Fiber 5g); Protein 7g.

FRUITED CHICKEN-RICE SALAD WITH TOASTED ALMONDS: *Decrease rice to 1 1/2 cups. Add 1 1/2 cups cubed cooked chicken or turkey with remaining ingredients in step 2. Continue as directed.*

Munchies to Have on Hand

- Assorted raw vegetables
- Cheese and whole grain crackers
- Chips and salsa
- Dips and spreads
- Dried fruit
- Fresh fruit

- Fruit-filled breakfast bars
- Popcorn
- Popcorn or rice cakes
- Pretzels
- Yogurt
- Hummus

Corn and Black Bean Salad with Tortilla Wedges

PREP: 15 min; BAKE: 4 min

4 SERVINGS

If you're eliminating all animal products from your diet, be certain to check tortilla labels; some tortillas may contain lard, which is animal fat. Whole wheat tortillas also make tasty wedges to serve with this salad.

4 fat-free flour tortillas (8 to 10 inches in diameter)

2 teaspoons margarine or butter, softened

1 can (15 to 16 ounces) whole kernel corn, drained

1 can (15 ounces) black beans, rinsed and drained

1 medium red bell pepper, chopped (1 cup)

1 small jicama, peeled and diced (2 cups)

1/2 cup fat-free Italian dressing

1/2 teaspoon salt

1/4 teaspoon pepper

Red leaf lettuce

1/4 cup pine nuts, toasted (page 18)

1. Heat oven to 400°. Spread tortillas with margarine; cut into fourths. Place on ungreased cookie sheet. Bake 4 to 5 minutes or until golden brown.

2. Toss remaining ingredients except lettuce and nuts until mixture is coated with dressing.

3. Serve salad on leaf lettuce; sprinkle with nuts. Serve with tortilla wedges.

1 Serving: Calories 285 (Calories from Fat 70); Fat 8g (Saturated 2g); Cholesterol 0mg; Sodium 1110mg; Carbohydrate 55g (Dietary Fiber 14g); Protein 12g.

> CORN AND BLACK BEAN SALAD WITH GRILLED CHICKEN: *Diagonally slice 4 grilled boneless, skinless chicken breast halves. Arrange chicken on salad in step 3. Continue as directed.*

Corn and Black Bean Salad with Tortilla Wedges and Couscous-Stuffed Avocados (page 100)

Bean and Spinach Salad with Warm Bell Pepper Dressing

PREP: 12 min; COOK: 3 min

4 SERVINGS

Cannellini beans are large white kidney beans that are widely used in Italian cuisine. They are soft-textured and very mild in flavor. If you don't have garlic pepper use 1/4 teaspoon garlic powder and 1/8 teaspoon pepper.

1 package (10 ounces) washed fresh spinach

1 can (15 to 16 ounces) cannellini beans, rinsed and drained

1 large bell pepper, coarsely chopped (1 1/2 cups)

2/3 cup fat-free Italian dressing

1/4 teaspoon garlic pepper

1 cup shredded mozzarella cheese (4 ounces)

1. Remove large stems from spinach; tear spinach into bite-size pieces. Place spinach in large bowl. Add beans; set aside.

2. Heat bell pepper and dressing to boiling in 1-quart saucepan; reduce heat. Cook uncovered 2 minutes, stirring occasionally. Stir in garlic pepper.

3. Pour bell pepper mixture over spinach and beans; toss. Sprinkle with cheese. Serve warm.

1 Serving: Calories 225 (Calories from Fat 55); Fat 6g (Saturated 4g); Cholesterol 15mg; Sodium 790mg; Carbohydrate 32g (Dietary Fiber 8g); Protein 19g.

> TUNA AND SPINACH SALAD WITH WARM BELL PEPPER DRESSING: *Add 1 can (6 ounces) tuna in water, drained, with beans in step 1. Increase Italian dressing to 3/4 cup in step 2. Continue as directed.*

Warm Tuscan Bean Salad

PREP: 15 min; COOK: 12 min

4 SERVINGS

If you just love the taste of crisp, smoky bacon but have dropped it from your diet, why not try bacon flavor bits? These bits are made from soybeans and contain no animal products but still have that salty, smoky flavor you crave.

1 tablespoon olive or vegetable oil

2 medium carrots, sliced (1 cup)

1 medium onion, chopped (1/2 cup)

2 cans (15 to 19 ounces each) cannellini beans, drained and 1/2 cup liquid reserved

1 1/2 teaspoons chopped fresh or 1/2 teaspoon dried oregano leaves

1/4 teaspoon pepper

4 cups bite-size pieces spinach leaves

1/4 cup red wine vinaigrette or Italian dressing

2 tablespoons bacon flavor bits

1. Heat oil in 12-inch skillet over medium heat. Cook carrots and onion in oil 5 to 7 minutes, stirring occasionally, until vegetables are crisp-tender.

2. Stir in beans, 1/2 cup reserved liquid, the oregano and pepper. Cook 5 minutes, stirring occasionally.

3. Line large platter with spinach. Top with bean mixture. Pour vinaigrette over salad. Sprinkle with bacon bits.

1 Serving: Calories 405 (Calories from Fat 100); Fat 11g (Saturated 2g); Cholesterol 2mg; Sodium 790mg; Carbohydrate 68g (Dietary Fiber 18g); Protein 26g.

WARM TUSCAN BEAN AND CHICKEN SALAD: *Omit 1 can of cannellini beans. Add 1 1/2 cups cubed cooked chicken or turkey with beans in step 2. Continue as directed.*

Black Bean Taco Salad

PREP: 12 min

4 SERVINGS

Convenience foods can be a trade-off—they cost more, but save time. The choice is yours. For example, shredded cheeses are widely available and extremely handy to keep in the refrigerator. Even though they cost more, they save you time. If you don't have any cumin on hand use chili powder.

2 cans (15 ounces each) black beans, rinsed and drained

1 can (2 1/4 ounces) sliced ripe olives, drained

2 medium tomatoes, chopped (1 1/2 cups)

4 medium green onions, chopped (1/4 cup)

1/3 cup shredded Cheddar cheese

1/4 cup chopped fresh cilantro

2 tablespoons lime juice

1 teaspoon ground cumin

1/4 teaspoon pepper

4 cups chopped spinach (6 ounces)

1. Mix beans, olives, tomatoes, onions, cheese and cilantro in a large bowl.

2. Mix lime juice, cumin and pepper; toss with bean mixture. Serve on spinach.

1 Serving: Calories 300 (Calories from Fat 55); Fat 6g (Saturated 3g); Cholesterol 10mg; Sodium 660mg; Carbohydrate 56g (Dietary Fiber 16g); Protein 21g.

CHICKEN TACO SALAD: *Omit 1 can of black beans. Add 1 1/2 cups chopped cooked chicken or turkey with the beans in step 1. Continue as directed.*

Mediterranean Salad

PREP: 12 min

4 SERVINGS

This salad is very pretty to look at and equally tasty to eat. Serve with crusty rolls and iced tea. For a flavor twist, sprinkle with crumbled feta, blue cheese or Gorgonzola cheese.

2 medium oranges

2/3 cup finely chopped red bell pepper

1/2 cup shredded fresh spinach

2 tablespoons halved pitted Kalamata or ripe olives

1 can (15 to 16 ounces) great northern beans, rinsed and drained

3 tablespoons red wine vinegar

2 tablespoons olive or vegetable oil

1/8 teaspoon pepper

1 clove garlic, finely chopped

1. Peel oranges and remove membrane; cut oranges into 1-inch pieces. Mix oranges, bell pepper, spinach, olives and beans in medium bowl.

2. Shake remaining ingredients in tightly covered container. Pour over orange mixture; toss.

1 Serving: Calories 210 (Calories from Fat 70); Fat 8g (Saturated 1g); Cholesterol 0mg; Sodium 270mg; Carbohydrate 33g (Dietary Fiber 8g); Protein 10g

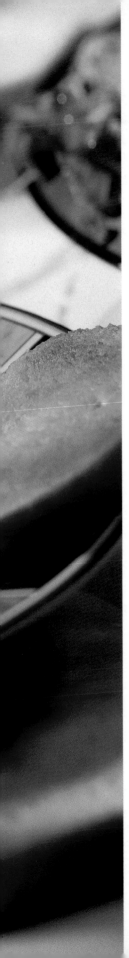

4

Easy Skillet Meals

Spaghetti and Spicy Rice Balls (page 133)

Steamed Vegetables in Peanut Sauce with Rice

PREP: 20 min; COOK: 10 min

4 SERVINGS

Treat yourself to basmati rice! Used extensively in Indian and Middle Eastern cooking, it has a heady, nutty aroma and flavor unmatched in any other variety of rice. The grains cook up very fluffy and stay separate.

1 Japanese or regular eggplant, cut into
   2 × 1/2-inch strips (3 cups)

1 medium red bell pepper, cut into julienne
   strips (1 1/2 cups)

1 large carrot, cut into julienne strips
   (1 cup)

1 cup sliced bok choy (stems and leaves)
   or celery

1 medium onion, thinly sliced

1/2 pound Chinese pea pods (2 cups)

2 tablespoons soy sauce

1 tablespoon creamy peanut butter

1 tablespoon hoisin sauce

1 teaspoon grated gingerroot

1 clove garlic, finely chopped

2 cups hot cooked basmati or other
   white rice

1. Place steamer basket in 1/2 inch water in saucepan or skillet (water should not touch bottom of basket). Place eggplant, bell pepper, carrot, bok choy and onion in steamer basket. Cover tightly and heat to boiling; reduce heat. Steam 5 to 8 minutes or until vegetables are crisp-tender; add pea pods for the last minute of steaming.

2. Beat soy sauce, peanut butter, hoisin sauce, gingerroot and garlic in large bowl, using wire whisk, until blended. Add vegetables to peanut butter mixture; toss. Serve over rice.

1 Serving: Calories 205 (Calories from Fat 25); Fat 3g (Saturated 1g); Cholesterol 0mg; Sodium 560mg; Carbohydrate 43g (Dietary Fiber 6g); Protein 7g.

Vegetable Jambalaya

PREP: 10 min; COOK: 35 min

4 SERVINGS

Serve this hearty main dish with corn muffins and sliced fresh fruit and garnish the jambalaya with chopped fresh parsley. If you like a little more kick to your jambalaya, sprinkle with red pepper sauce or your favorite hot sauce.

1 tablespoon vegetable oil

1 large onion, coarsely chopped (1 cup)

1 medium green bell pepper, coarsely chopped (1 cup)

2 cloves garlic, finely chopped

1 cup uncooked regular long grain rice

1 can (14 1/2 ounces) ready-to-serve vegetable broth

1 cup frozen whole kernel corn

2 tablespoons Worcestershire sauce

1/8 teaspoon ground red pepper (cayenne)

1 can (15 to 16 ounces) black-eyed peas, rinsed and drained

1 can (14 1/2 ounces) stewed tomatoes, undrained

1. Heat oil in 10-inch skillet over medium-high heat. Cook onion, bell pepper and garlic in oil 3 to 5 minutes, stirring occasionally, until vegetables are crisp-tender.

2. Stir in rice. Cook 2 to 3 minutes, stirring occasionally, until rice is light golden brown. Stir in broth. Heat to boiling; reduce heat to low. Cover and simmer 15 minutes.

3. Stir in remaining ingredients. Cover and simmer 5 to 10 minutes or until vegetables and rice are tender.

1 Serving: Calories 395 (Calories from Fat 45); Fat 5g (Saturated 2g); Cholesterol 0mg; Sodium 1030mg; Carbohydrate 83g (Dietary Fiber 10g); Protein 14g.

VEGETABLE JAMBALAYA WITH HAM: *Add 1/2 cup diced turkey ham with remaining ingredients in step 3. Continue as directed.*

Vegetable Paella

PREP: 7 min; COOK: 15 min

4 SERVINGS

Saffron gives paella its characteristic bright yellow color and distinct flavor, but it can be expensive. Turmeric can be substituted for the saffron.

2 tablespoons olive or vegetable oil

2 cloves garlic, finely chopped

1 large red onion, cut into thin wedges

1 cup uncooked quick-cooking brown rice

1 cup vegetable or chicken broth

1/2 teaspoon saffron threads, crushed

1 package (16 ounces) frozen sweet peas, potatoes and carrots

1 can (14 1/2 ounces) stewed tomatoes, undrained

1. Heat oil in 12-inch nonstick skillet over medium-high heat. Cook garlic and onion in oil, stirring frequently, until onion is tender.

2. Stir in remaining ingredients. Heat to boiling; reduce heat to medium-low. Cover and cook 5 minutes, stirring occasionally; remove from heat. Let stand covered 5 minutes.

1 Serving: Calories 355 (Calories from Fat 80); Fat 9g (Saturated 2g); Cholesterol 0mg; Sodium 600mg; Carbohydrate 67g (Dietary Fiber 8g); Protein 9g.

VEGETABLE CHICKEN PAELLA: *Add 1 cup cubed cooked chicken or turkey with remaining ingredients in step 2. Continue as directed.*

Moroccan Vegetables

PREP: 15 min; COOK: 9 min

4 SERVINGS

You can use 1 1/2 teaspoons of curry powder in place of the cumin, turmeric, cinnamon and pepper. There are two types of commercial curry powder available: standard and a hotter version known as "Madras."

2 teaspoons vegetable oil

2 medium carrots, sliced (1 cup)

1 large onion, chopped (1 cup)

1 large red bell pepper, cut into 3/4-inch pieces (1 cup)

2 cloves garlic, finely chopped

1/2 cup raisins

1 teaspoon ground cumin

1/2 teaspoon salt

1/4 teaspoon ground turmeric

1/4 teaspoon ground cinnamon

1/8 teaspoon pepper

1 small zucchini, sliced (1 cup)

1 can (15 to 16 ounces) garbanzo beans, rinsed and drained

2 tablespoons chopped fresh parsley

Hot cooked couscous or rice, if desired

1. Heat oil in 12-inch nonstick skillet over medium-high heat. Cook carrots, onion, bell pepper and garlic in oil about 4 minutes, stirring frequently, until onion is tender.

2. Stir in remaining ingredients except parsley and couscous. Cook about 5 minutes, stirring frequently, until zucchini is tender. Sprinkle with parsley. Serve over couscous.

1 Serving: Calories 235 (Calories from Fat 45); Fat 5g (Saturated 1g); Cholesterol 0mg; Sodium 490mg; Carbohydrate 46g (Dietary Fiber 7g); Protein 8g.

Vegetable Curry with Couscous

PREP: 10 min; COOK: 12 min

4 SERVINGS

Because curry powder is a mixture of spices, the flavor will vary with the brand. Experimenting with different brands of curry powder can be an exciting culinary adventure.

1 tablespoon vegetable oil

1 medium red bell pepper, cut into thin strips

1/4 cup vegetable or chicken broth

1 tablespoon curry powder

1 teaspoon salt

1 package (16 ounces) frozen broccoli, carrots and cauliflower

1/2 cup raisins

1/3 cup chutney

2 cups hot cooked couscous or rice

1/4 cup chopped peanuts

1. Heat oil in 12-inch skillet over medium-high heat. Cook bell pepper in oil, stirring frequently, until tender.

2. Stir in broth, curry powder, salt and vegetables. Heat to boiling. Boil about 4 minutes, stirring frequently, until vegetables are crisp-tender.

3. Stir in raisins and chutney. Serve over couscous. Sprinkle with peanuts.

1 Serving: Calories 290 (Calories from Fat 70); Fat 8g (Saturated 2g); Cholesterol 0mg; Sodium 950mg; Carbohydrate 53g (Dietary Fiber 7g); Protein 9g.

> CHICKEN CURRY WITH COUSCOUS: *Add 2 skinless, boneless chicken breast halves, cut into 3/4-inch pieces with the bell pepper in step 1. Cook until chicken is no longer pink. Continue as directed.*

Vegetable Curry with Couscous

Easy Vegetable Chow Mein

PREP: 5 min; COOK: 10 min

4 SERVINGS

Use the frozen stir-fry vegetables suggested in this recipe, or try using one of your favorite frozen stir-fry vegetable combinations. Oyster sauce is a thick brown sauce made from oysters, salt and starch. If oyster sauce isn't available, use one tablespoon soy sauce instead.

1 cup vegetable or chicken broth

2 tablespoons cornstarch

2 tablespoons oyster sauce

1/4 teaspoon red pepper sauce

2 tablespoons vegetable oil

2 cloves garlic, finely chopped

1 package (16 ounces) frozen snap peas, carrots, onions and mushrooms

2 1/2 cups coleslaw mix

4 cups chow mein noodles

1. Mix broth, cornstarch, oyster sauce and pepper sauce; set aside.

2. Heat oil in 12-inch nonstick skillet over medium-high heat. Cook garlic and frozen vegetables in oil about 5 minutes, stirring frequently, until vegetables are crisp-tender.

3. Stir in coleslaw mix and broth mixture. Cook, stirring constantly, until thickened. Serve over noodles.

1 Serving: Calories 380 (Calories from Fat 190); Fat 21g (Saturated 3g); Cholesterol 0mg; Sodium 870mg; Carbohydrate 46g (Dietary Fiber 7g); Protein 9g.

EASY CHICKEN CHOW MEIN: *Add 2 cups cubed cooked chicken or turkey with frozen vegetables in step 2. Continue as directed.*

Caramelized-Vegetable Medley

PREP: 15 min; COOK: 22 min

4 SERVINGS

Serve this rich, flavorful vegetable dish with a hearty bread, or serve it over pasta, such as penne or mostaccioli. Top it with a sprinkle of shredded smoked Gouda cheese for extra flavor.

1/4 cup margarine or butter

**2 medium onions, sliced and separated
into rings**

8 small red potatoes, cut in half

2 tablespoons packed brown sugar

1/2 pound whole mushrooms

1 teaspoon dried thyme leaves

2 tablespoons cider vinegar

1/2 teaspoon salt

2 cups thin strips spinach leaves

1 medium tomato, chopped (3/4 cup)

1. Melt margarine in 12-inch nonstick skillet over medium heat. Cook onions, potatoes and brown sugar in margarine 12 minutes, stirring frequently.

2. Stir in mushrooms and thyme. Cook 7 minutes, stirring frequently, until potatoes are tender.

3. Stir in vinegar and salt. Add spinach and tomato; toss. Cook 1 minute.

1 Serving: Calories 295 (Calories from Fat 110); Fat 12g (Saturated 8g); Cholesterol 30mg; Sodium 410mg; Carbohydrate 47g (Dietary Fiber 5g); Protein 5g.

Bok Choy and Cashew Stir-Fry

PREP: 10 min; COOK: 7 min

4 SERVINGS

Bok choy is a leafy green vegetable that resembles celery in shape but has white stalks and dark green leaves. The leaves are often separated and added after the stalks are cooked, to prevent overcooking.

1/2 cup vegetable or chicken broth

2 tablespoons soy sauce

4 teaspoons cornstarch

6 stalks bok choy

2 tablespoons vegetable oil

1 large onion, sliced and separated
   into rings

2 cloves garlic, finely chopped

1 teaspoon finely chopped gingerroot

1/2 pound mushrooms, cut in half

1/2 cup whole cashews or peanuts

1. Mix broth, soy sauce and cornstarch; set aside. Separate bok choy leaves from stems. Cut leaves and stems into 1-inch pieces.

2. Heat oil in 12-inch nonstick skillet or wok over medium-high heat. Add bok choy stems, onion, garlic and gingerroot; stirring constantly cook 2 minutes. Stir in bok choy leaves and mushrooms. Cook 1 minute, stirring constantly.

3. Stir in broth mixture. Cook, stirring constantly, about 4 minutes or until thickened. Stir in cashews.

1 Serving: Calories 225 (Calories from Fat 145); Fat 16g (Saturated 3g); Cholesterol 0mg; Sodium 810mg; Carbohydrate 17g (Dietary Fiber 3g); Protein 6g.

CHICKEN BOK CHOY AND CASHEW STIR-FRY: *Add 1 cup cubed cooked chicken or turkey with bok choy stems in step 2. Continue as directed.*

Mixed Mushroom Stroganoff

PREP: 11 min; COOK: 8 min

6 SERVINGS

This meatless stroganoff is just as hearty as its beef counterpart, thanks to the mushrooms. Look for and experiment with the many mushroom varieties now available.

1/4 cup margarine or butter

2 cloves garlic, finely chopped

1 large onion, sliced and separated into rings

1 pound assorted mushrooms (portobello, crimini, oyster or button), sliced

1 tablespoon chopped fresh parsley

1 teaspoon dried sage leaves

1/2 teaspoon salt

1 cup vegetable or chicken broth

2 tablespoons all-purpose flour

1 cup sour cream

6 cups hot cooked egg noodles

Chopped fresh parsley

1. Melt margarine in 12-inch skillet over medium-high heat. Cook garlic, onion and mushrooms in margarine, stirring occasionally, until tender. Stir in 1 tablespoon parsley, the sage and salt.

2. Mix broth and flour; stir into mushroom mixture. Heat to boiling. Boil, stirring constantly, until thickened; reduce heat to low.

3. Stir in sour cream (do not boil). Serve over noodles. Sprinkle with parsley.

1 Serving: Calories 395 (Calories from Fat 160); Fat 18g (Saturated 10g); Cholesterol 100mg; Sodium 440mg; Carbohydrate 50g (Dietary Fiber 3g); Protein 11g.

Hot German Potato and Bean Skillet Dinner

PREP: 2 min; COOK: 10 min

4 SERVINGS

Vegetarians often substitute arrowroot for cornstarch. Arrowroot, the fine powder from the tropical arrowroot tuber, has no flavor and becomes clear when cooked. Unlike cornstarch, arrowroot doesn't taste chalky when undercooked.

2 tablespoons vegetable oil

1 package (16 ounces) frozen green beans, potatoes, onions and red peppers

2/3 cup vegetable or chicken broth

1/3 cup cider vinegar

1 tablespoon sugar

1 tablespoon cornstarch

1 can (15 to 16 ounces) kidney beans, rinsed and drained

1 can (15 to 16 ounces) garbanzo beans, rinsed and drained

2 tablespoons bacon flavor bits or chips, if desired

1. Heat oil in 12-inch nonstick skillet over medium-high heat. Cook vegetables in oil about 5 minutes, stirring frequently, until hot.

2. Mix broth, vinegar, sugar and cornstarch; stir into vegetables. Heat to boiling. Boil, stirring constantly, until thickened.

3. Stir in beans. Cook until beans are hot. Sprinkle with bacon bits.

1 Serving: Calories 285 (Calories from Fat 80); Fat 9g (Saturated 2g); Cholesterol 0mg; Sodium 660mg; Carbohydrate 49g (Dietary Fiber 11g); Protein 13g.

West African Sweet Potato Supper

PREP: 10 min; COOK: 23 min

6 SERVINGS

To make peeling the sweet potatoes easier, microwave potatoes on High for two minutes first. For a nice color contrast, try a can of black beans instead of the great northern beans.

1 tablespoon vegetable oil

1 medium onion, sliced and separated
    into rings

1/4 cup creamy peanut butter

1 teaspoon chili powder

1/2 teaspoon ground ginger

1/2 teaspoon salt

1/4 teaspoon ground red pepper (cayenne)

3 large sweet potatoes, peeled and cut into
    1/2-inch cubes (4 cups)

2 cans (14 1/2 ounces each) diced tomatoes
    with roasted garlic, undrained

1 can (15 to 16 ounces) great northern
    beans, undrained

1 can (15 1/4 ounces) whole kernel corn,
    drained

Hot cooked couscous or rice, if desired

1. Heat oil in 4-quart Dutch oven over medium-high heat. Cook onion in oil, stirring frequently, until tender.

2. Stir in remaining ingredients except couscous. Heat to boiling; reduce heat to medium-low. Cover and cook about 20 to 25 minutes, stirring occasionally, until potatoes are tender. Serve over couscous.

1 Serving: Calories 340 (Calories from Fat 80); Fat 9g (Saturated 2g); Cholesterol 0mg; Sodium 870mg; Carbohydrate 62g (Dietary Fiber 11g); Protein 14g.

WEST AFRICAN SWEET POTATO CHICKEN SUPPER: *Add 2 skinless, boneless chicken breast halves, cut into 3/4-inch pieces, with the onion in step 1. Cook until chicken is no longer pink. Continue as directed.*

Fresh Spinach and New Potato Frittata

PREP: 15 min; COOK: 20 min

4 SERVINGS

Purchase spinach that has already been washed to speed the preparation of this tasty dish—it's perfect for breakfast, lunch or dinner. Use sliced jarred pimiento to add color if sun-dried tomatoes aren't available.

2 tablespoons margarine or butter

6 or 7 small red potatoes, thinly sliced
   (2 cups)

3 medium green onions, cut into
   1/4-inch pieces

1/4 teaspoon salt

1 cup firmly packed bite-size pieces spinach

1/4 cup oil-packed sun-dried tomatoes,
   drained and sliced

6 eggs

2 tablespoons milk

1/4 teaspoon dried marjoram leaves

1/4 teaspoon salt

1/2 cup shredded Swiss cheese (2 ounces)

1. Melt margarine in 10-inch nonstick skillet over medium heat. Add potatoes, onions and 1/4 teaspoon salt. Cover and cook 8 to 10 minutes, stirring occasionally, until potatoes are tender.

2. Stir in spinach and tomatoes. Cook, stirring occasionally, just until spinach is wilted; reduce heat to low.

3. Beat eggs, milk, marjoram and 1/4 teaspoon salt. Carefully pour over potato mixture. Cover and cook 6 to 8 minutes or just until top is set. Sprinkle with cheese. Cover and cook about 1 minute or until cheese is melted.

1 Serving: Calories 360 (Calories from Fat 165); Fat 18g (Saturated 7g); Cholesterol 330mg; Sodium 530mg; Carbohydrate 37g (Dietary Fiber 4g); Protein 17g.

Wild Rice Frittata

PREP: 10 min; COOK: 25 min; STAND: 5 min

6 SERVINGS

This frittata, or Italian omelet, is a hassle-free way to cook eggs. No stirring or flipping—just set the timer and go! We have eliminated the traditional step of flipping the frittata out of the skillet and returning it to the skillet to finish cooking. If you like, use cooked white or brown rice instead of the wild rice.

1 tablespoon margarine or butter

1 small green bell pepper, chopped (1/2 cup)

1 small red bell pepper, chopped (1/2 cup)

1 medium onion, chopped (1/2 cup)

6 eggs, beaten

1/4 cup milk

1 cup cooked wild rice

1 cup shredded Swiss cheese (4 ounces)

1. Melt margarine in 10-inch nonstick skillet over medium heat. Cook bell peppers and onion in margarine, stirring frequently, until vegetables are crisp-tender.

2. Mix eggs, milk, wild rice and 1/2 cup of the cheese. Pour egg mixture over vegetables; reduce heat. Cover and cook 15 to 20 minutes or until eggs are set; remove from heat.

3. Sprinkle with remaining 1/2 cup cheese. Cover and let stand about 5 minutes or until cheese is melted. Serve immediately.

1 Serving: Calories 195 (Calories from Fat 110); Fat 12g (Saturated 6g); Cholesterol 230mg; Sodium 140mg; Carbohydrate 10g (Dietary Fiber 1g); Protein 13g.

Denver Eggs Frittata

PREP: 6 min; COOK: 16 min; STAND: 2 min

4 SERVINGS

Frittata is the Italian word for "omelet." A frittata differs from a traditional omelet in several ways: The frittata filling becomes part of the egg mixture, rather than a filling, and additional ingredients may be sprinkled on top. Also, the traditional way to serve a frittata is to cut it into wedges.

2 tablespoons vegetable oil

1/2 medium green bell pepper, cut into 1-inch strips

1/2 medium red bell pepper, cut into 1-inch strips

1 medium onion, sliced

8 eggs

1/2 teaspoon salt

1 can (1 1/2 ounces) shoestring potatoes

1/2 cup shredded Cheddar cheese (2 ounces)

1. Heat oil in 12-inch nonstick skillet over medium-high heat. Cook bell peppers and onion in oil about 5 minutes, stirring occasionally, until tender. Spread vegetables evenly in skillet.

2. Beat eggs and salt. Pour eggs over vegetables; reduce heat to low. Cover and cook 7 to 9 minutes or until eggs are set; remove from heat.

3. Sprinkle with potatoes and cheese. Cover and let stand about 2 minutes or until cheese is melted. Cut into wedges.

1 Serving: Calories 345 (Calories from Fat 235); Fat 26g (Saturated 9g); Cholesterol 440mg; Sodium 540mg; Carbohydrate 12g (Dietary Fiber 1g); Protein 17g.

Denver Eggs Frittata

Tex-Mex Scrambled Eggs

PREP: 10 min; COOK: 10 min
4 SERVINGS

It's easy to replace meat with eggs as a source of protein, but if you're watching your cholesterol, you may want to substitute fat-free cholesterol-free egg product in this recipe. One-fourth cup of egg substitute equals one whole egg.

2 teaspoons vegetable oil

3 corn tortillas (5 or 6 inches in diameter), cut into thin strips

1 small onion, chopped (1/4 cup)

8 eggs, beaten

1/2 medium jalapeño chili, seeded and chopped

1 cup salsa

1/4 cup sour cream

2 medium green onions, chopped (2 tablespoons)

1. Heat oil in 10-inch nonstick skillet over medium-high heat. Cook tortilla strips and 1/4 cup onion in oil about 5 minutes, stirring frequently, until tortillas are crisp. Mix eggs and chili; pour over tortilla mixture. Reduce heat to medium.

2. As mixture begins to set at bottom and side, gently lift cooked portions with spatula so that thin, uncooked portion can flow to bottom. Do not stir. Cook 4 to 5 minutes or until eggs are set but still moist.

3. Top each serving with salsa, sour cream and green onions.

1 Serving: Calories 255 (Calories from Fat 145); Fat 16g (Saturated 6g); Cholesterol 430mg; Sodium 330mg; Carbohydrate 16g (Dietary Fiber 3g); Protein 15g.

Vegetable Poached Eggs

PREP: 15 min; COOK: 17 min

4 SERVINGS

Pull out this recipe when you'd like to prepare a casual brunch dish; not only is it attractive, it's full of flavor, too. The eggs may be firmer than expected, but this doneness ensures that the eggs are safe to eat.

2 cups chopped broccoli

2 cups chopped spinach (3 ounces)

1 cup sliced mushrooms (3 ounces)

1 large onion, chopped (1 cup)

1 medium carrot, cut into julienne strips (1/2 cup)

1 small zucchini, cut into julienne strips (1/2 cup)

3/4 cup marinara sauce or spaghetti sauce

1/4 teaspoon pepper

4 eggs

1/4 cup shredded mozzarella cheese (1 ounce)

1. Spray 12-inch skillet with cooking spray; heat over medium heat. Cook broccoli, spinach, mushrooms, onion, carrot and zucchini in skillet 8 to 10 minutes, stirring occasionally, until vegetables are crisp-tender.

2. Stir in marinara sauce and pepper. Cook, stirring constantly, until hot.

3. Make four 3-inch indentations in vegetable mixture, using back of large spoon. Break 1 egg into each indentation. Cover and cook about 5 minutes or until egg whites and yolks are firm, not runny. Sprinkle with cheese. Serve immediately.

1 Serving: Calories 185 (Calories from Fat 70); Fat 8g (Saturated 3g); Cholesterol 220mg; Sodium 370mg; Carbohydrate 20g (Dietary Fiber 4g); Protein 12g.

Pan-Roasted Garden Vegetables with Eggs

PREP: 5 min; COOK: 15 min

4 SERVINGS

Italian blend cheese is a packaged preshredded blend of six different cheeses: Asiago, fontina, mozzarella, Parmesan, provolone and Romano. If you like, shredded Parmesan cheese can be used in place of the Italian blend cheese.

3 tablespoons olive or vegetable oil

1 cup sliced mushrooms (3 ounces)

1/2 medium onion, cut into wedges

1 package (1 pound 10 ounces) frozen roasted potatoes, broccoli, cauliflower and carrots with Parmesan and Romano seasonings

4 eggs

1/2 cup shredded Italian-style six-cheese blend (2 ounces)

1. Heat oil in 12-inch nonstick skillet over medium-high heat. Add mushrooms, onion and frozen vegetables. Sprinkle with contents of seasoning packet from frozen vegetables; stir to coat vegetables. Cook 6 minutes, stirring constantly.

2. Make 4 indentations in vegetable mixture. Break 1 egg into each indentation; reduce heat to medium-low. Cover and cook 6 to 9 minutes or until egg whites and yolks are firm, not runny.

3. Sprinkle with cheese. Cover and cook about 1 minute or until cheese is melted.

1 Serving: Calories 365 (Calories from Fat 180); Fat 20g (Saturated 6g); Cholesterol 225mg; Sodium 800mg; Carbohydrate 35g (Dietary Fiber 5g); Protein 16g.

Tropical Pasta

PREP: 15 min; COOK: 20 min

4 SERVINGS

This smashing fusion of flavors deserves your attention. For an absolutely stunning presentation, serve on solid black plates. No papaya? Use a cup of chopped fresh or canned peaches.

4 ounces uncooked vermicelli

**1 medium red bell pepper, cut into
2 × 1/4-inch strips**

1 small papaya or mango, chopped (1 cup)

1 medium tomato, chopped (3/4 cup)

2 tablespoons chopped fresh cilantro

1 tablespoon peanut oil

1/2 teaspoon salt

1/2 teaspoon ground cardamom

1/4 cup cocktail peanuts, chopped

1. Cook and drain vermicelli as directed on package. Rinse with cold water; drain.

2. Toss vermicelli and remaining ingredients except peanuts. Sprinkle with peanuts.

1 Serving: Calories 210 (Calories from Fat 70); Fat 8g
(Saturated 1g); Cholesterol 0mg; Sodium 300mg;
Carbohydrate 31g (Dietary Fiber 3g); Protein 6g.

Spaghetti with Golden Onions

PREP: 10 min; COOK: 20 min

6 SERVINGS

Your taste buds will appreciate the explosion of flavors in this sophisticated spaghetti. Serve it for a casual get-together with a simple tossed salad and a crunchy baguette.

8 ounces uncooked spaghetti

1 tablespoon olive or vegetable oil

1 tablespoon margarine or butter

4 large onions, coarsely chopped (4 cups)

1/2 teaspoon dried thyme leaves

**1/4 teaspoon dried rosemary leaves,
crumbled**

1 cup frozen (thawed) green peas

1 medium tomato, chopped (3/4 cup)

2 tablespoons balsamic vinegar

1/2 teaspoon salt

1. Cook and drain spaghetti as directed on package.

2. While spaghetti is cooking, heat oil and margarine in 10-inch skillet over medium heat. Cook onions, thyme and rosemary in oil mixture 12 to 15 minutes, stirring occasionally, until onions are deep golden brown and tender. Stir in peas, tomato, vinegar and salt. Toss with spaghetti.

1 Serving: Calories 230 (Calories from Fat 45); Fat 5g
(Saturated 1g); Cholesterol 0mg; Sodium 240mg;
Carbohydrate 43g (Dietary Fiber 4g); Protein 7g.

Broccoli-Mushroom Spaghetti

PREP: 5 min; COOK: 15 min

4 SERVINGS

Adding the broccoli to the spaghetti while it is cooking is a slick, quick-cooking trick that works for any pasta vegetable combination that's tossed together after cooking.

1 package (7 ounces) spaghetti

1 package (10 ounces) frozen chopped
   broccoli, rinsed to separate

1 jar (4 1/2 ounces) sliced mushrooms,
   drained

1/4 cup margarine or butter

1/2 teaspoon salt

1/8 teaspoon pepper

1/2 cup grated Parmesan cheese

1 tablespoon lemon juice

1. Cook spaghetti as directed on package, except add broccoli about 5 minutes before spaghetti is done; drain.

2. Stir mushrooms, margarine, salt and pepper into spaghetti and broccoli. Cook over low heat about 5 minutes, stirring occasionally, until mushrooms are hot. Sprinkle with cheese and lemon juice; toss.

1 Serving: Calories 360 (Calories from Fat 145); Fat 16g (Saturated 5g); Cholesterol 10mg; Sodium 740mg; Carbohydrate 45g (Dietary Fiber 4g); Protein 13g.

BROCCOLI-TUNA SPAGHETTI: *Add 1 can (6 ounces) tuna in water, drained, with broccoli in step 2. Continue as directed.*

Spaghetti and Spicy Rice Balls

PREP: 12 min; COOK: 15 min

6 SERVINGS

Rice and oats replace ground beef in these "meatballs." They are rolled in a small amount of wheat germ to give them a golden brown color and just a bit of crunch. Wheat germ has a nutty flavor and is very oily, which causes it to turn rancid quickly. It is best to store it in the refrigerator.

1 package (16 ounces) uncooked spaghetti

2 cups cooked white rice

1/2 cup quick-cooking oats

1 medium onion, chopped (1/2 cup)

1/4 cup dry bread crumbs

1/4 cup milk

1 tablespoon chopped fresh or 1 teaspoon dried basil leaves

2 teaspoons chopped fresh or 1/2 teaspoon dried oregano leaves

1/4 teaspoon ground red pepper (cayenne)

1 egg, beaten

1/2 cup wheat germ

1 tablespoon vegetable oil

2 cups prepared spaghetti sauce

Finely shredded Parmesan cheese, if desired

1. Cook spaghetti as directed on package; drain.

2. While spaghetti is cooking, mix rice, oats, onion, bread crumbs, milk, basil, oregano, red pepper and egg. Shape mixture into 10 balls. Roll balls in wheat germ.

3. Heat oil in 10-inch skillet over medium heat. Cook balls in oil about 10 minutes, turning occasionally, until light golden brown.

4. Heat spaghetti sauce until hot. Serve sauce and rice balls over spaghetti; sprinkle with Parmesan cheese.

1 Serving: Calories 525 (Calories from Fat 90); Fat 10g (Saturated 2g); Cholesterol 38mg; Sodium 466mg; Carbohydrate 77g (Dietary Fiber 5g); Protein 13g.

Garden Vegetable Spaghetti

PREP: 20 min; COOK: 15 min

6 SERVINGS

Whole wheat pasta is light brown or tan when cooked and isn't as sticky as regular pasta. Another bonus of whole wheat pasta is its slightly nutty flavor and higher fiber content.

1 package (16 ounces) whole wheat or regular spaghetti

2 tablespoons olive or vegetable oil

2 medium carrots, sliced (2 cups)

1 medium onion, chopped (1/2 cup)

1 medium stalk celery, thinly sliced (1/2 cup)

1 small eggplant (3/4 pound), diced (3 1/2 cups)

1 clove garlic, finely chopped

1/2 cup frozen green peas

2 tablespoons chopped fresh parsley

1 1/2 teaspoons chopped fresh or 1/2 teaspoon dried basil leaves

3/4 teaspoon chopped fresh or 1/4 teaspoon dried tarragon leaves

1/2 teaspoon salt

1/4 teaspoon pepper

3 medium tomatoes, cut into 1-inch pieces

2/3 cup grated Parmesan cheese

1. Cook and drain spaghetti as directed on package.

2. While spaghetti is cooking, heat oil in 10-inch skillet over medium-high heat. Cook carrots, onion, celery, eggplant and garlic in oil, stirring frequently, until vegetables are crisp-tender.

3. Stir in remaining ingredients except cheese; cook until hot. Serve vegetable mixture over spaghetti. Sprinkle with cheese.

1 Serving: Calories 415 (Calories from Fat 80); Fat 9g (Saturated 3g); Cholesterol 5mg; Sodium 390mg; Carbohydrate 74g (Dietary Fiber 7g); Protein 16g.

Garden Vegetable Spaghetti and Fresh Mushroom Fettuccine (page 136)

Fresh Mushroom Fettuccine

PREP: 15 min; COOK: 13 min

4 SERVINGS

The chewy, meatlike texture of mushrooms makes them an excellent meat replacement. Some mushrooms, such as portobello, shiitake, oyster and porcini, have a meatier texture than regular white mushrooms.

8 ounces uncooked fettuccine

3 cups sliced mushrooms (1/2 pound)

1/4 cup chopped fresh parsley

1/4 cup freshly grated Parmesan cheese

1/4 cup red wine vinegar

1/4 cup olive or vegetable oil

2 teaspoons chopped fresh rosemary leaves

1/2 teaspoon freshly ground pepper

1/4 teaspoon salt

1 clove garlic, finely chopped

1. Cook and drain fettuccine as directed on package; return to pan.

2. Add remaining ingredients; toss until fettuccine is coated with oil.

1 Serving: Calories 350 (Calories from Fat 155); Fat 17g (Saturated 4g); Cholesterol 55mg; Sodium 250mg; Carbohydrate 41g (Dietary Fiber 2g); Protein 10g.

Fettuccine Primavera

PREP: 12 min; COOK: 10 min

4 SERVINGS

Look for the refrigerated Alfredo sauce next to the fresh pasta. If you're counting calories and fat, purchase the light variety. If you like, use linguine or spaghetti instead of the fettuccine.

8 ounces uncooked fettuccine

1 tablespoon olive or vegetable oil

1 cup broccoli flowerets

1 cup cauliflowerets

1 cup frozen green peas, rinsed to separate

2 medium carrots, thinly sliced (1 cup)

1 small onion, chopped (1/4 cup)

1 container (10 ounces) refrigerated Alfredo sauce

1 tablespoon grated Parmesan cheese

1. Cook and drain fettuccine as directed on package.

2. While fettuccine is cooking, heat oil in 12-inch skillet over medium-high heat. Cook broccoli, cauliflowerets, peas, carrots and onion in oil 6 to 8 minutes, stirring frequently, until vegetables are crisp-tender.

3. Stir Alfredo sauce into vegetable mixture; cook until hot. Stir in fettuccine; heat through. Sprinkle with cheese.

1 Serving: Calories 515 (Calories from Fat 260); Fat 29g (Saturated 16g); Cholesterol 120mg; Sodium 390mg; Carbohydrate 53g (Dietary Fiber 6g); Protein 16g.

Spring Vegetable Fettuccine

PREP: 3 min; COOK: 12 min

4 SERVINGS

This recipe is ready in no time flat, as it has time-savers such as fresh pasta and flavored, spreadable cheese. You may want to try different vegetable mixtures for variety.

1 package (9 ounces) refrigerated fettuccine

1 cup half-and-half

1 container (5 ounces) garlic-and-herb spreadable cheese

1/2 teaspoon garlic salt

1 package (16 ounces) frozen baby peas, carrots, pea pods and corn, thawed and drained

Freshly ground pepper, if desired

1. Cook and drain fettuccine as directed on package.

2. While fettuccine is cooking, heat half-and-half to boiling in 12-inch nonstick skillet over medium heat. Stir in cheese and garlic salt. Cook, stirring constantly, until cheese is melted and mixture is smooth.

3. Stir in vegetables. Cook, stirring occasionally, 7 minutes or until vegetables are tender. Serve over fettuccine. Sprinkle with pepper.

1 Serving: Calories 450 (Calories from Fat 190); Fat 21g (Saturated 12g); Cholesterol 115mg; Sodium 320mg; Carbohydrate 56g (Dietary Fiber 6g); Protein 15g.

SHRIMP VEGETABLE FETTUCCINE: *Add 1/2 pound cooked peeled shrimp, with vegetables in step 3. Continue as directed.*

Gorgonzola Linguine with Toasted Walnuts

PREP: 5 min; COOK: 20 min

4 SERVINGS

Certain foods just have a love affair with one another, and so it is with the combination of Gorgonzola and toasted walnuts. One taste of this heavenly combo and you will be hooked! Want the great taste in this recipe, but a few less calories and fat? Use nonfat half-and-half.

4 ounces uncooked linguine

1 tablespoon margarine or butter

1 clove garlic, finely chopped

3/4 cup half-and-half

1/4 cup dry white wine or vegetable broth

1/4 teaspoon salt

1/2 cup crumbled Gorgonzola cheese (2 ounces)

1/4 cup chopped walnuts, toasted (page 18)

1. Cook and drain linguine as directed on package.

2. While linguine is cooking, melt margarine in 2-quart saucepan over medium heat. Cook garlic in margarine, stirring occasionally, until golden brown. Stir in half-and-half, wine and salt. Cook, stirring occasionally, until mixture thickens slightly; reduce heat to medium-low. Stir in cheese. Cook, stirring occasionally, until cheese is melted.

3. Toss linguine and sauce. Sprinkle with walnuts.

1 Serving: Calories 305 (Calories from Fat 160); Fat 18g (Saturated 8g); Cholesterol 30mg; Sodium 440mg; Carbohydrate 27g (Dietary Fiber 1g); Protein 10g.

Peanut-Vegetable Lo Mein

PREP: 10 min; COOK: 25 min

4 SERVINGS

If cream of coconut is not available, increase the half-and-half to 1/3 cup and sprinkle the finished dish with peanuts and coconut. For added coconut flavor, toast the coconut. Sprinkle 1/2 cup coconut in an ungreased heavy skillet. Cook over medium-low heat 6 to 14 minutes, stirring frequently, until browning begins, then stir constantly until golden brown.

1 medium onion, cut into thin wedges

1 clove garlic, finely chopped

1 teaspoon finely chopped gingerroot

1 can (14 1/2 ounces) ready-to-serve vegetable broth

2 tablespoons soy sauce

1 package (16 ounces) fresh (refrigerated) stir-fry vegetables

1 1/2 cups uncooked fine egg noodles (3 ounces)

1/3 cup creamy peanut butter

3 tablespoons half-and-half

3 tablespoons cream of coconut or coconut milk

1/4 teaspoon crushed red pepper

2 tablespoons chopped peanuts

1. Spray 10-inch nonstick skillet with cooking spray; heat over medium heat. Cook onion, garlic and gingerroot in skillet 3 to 5 minutes, stirring occasionally, until onion is crisp-tender.

2. Stir in broth, soy sauce and vegetables. Heat to boiling; reduce heat to medium. Cover and cook about 5 minutes or until vegetables are tender.

3. Stir in noodles. Cover and cook 5 to 8 minutes, stirring occasionally, until liquid is almost absorbed.

4. Beat peanut butter, half-and-half, cream of coconut and red pepper, using wire whisk, until smooth. Stir into vegetable mixture. Cook over medium heat 3 to 5 minutes, stirring occasionally, until hot. Sprinkle with peanuts.

1 Serving: Calories 330 (Calories from Fat 170); Fat 19g (Saturated 8g); Cholesterol 25mg; Sodium 1070mg; Carbohydrate 33g (Dietary Fiber 6g); Protein 13g.

PEANUT-CHICKEN LO MEIN: *Add 2 skinless, boneless chicken breast halves, cut into 3/4-inch pieces, with the onion in step 1. Cook until chicken is no longer pink. Continue as directed.*

Mushrooms Paprikash

PREP: 8 min; COOK: 10 min

6 SERVINGS

Lots of mushrooms replace the traditional chicken in this inspired rendition of the Hungarian classic and paprika gives it a rich reddish color. Replace some of the popular white mushrooms with some wild mushrooms—chanterelle, morel, and shiitake are all good additions.

4 cups uncooked egg noodles (8 ounces)

1 tablespoon margarine or butter

2 packages (8 ounces each) sliced mushrooms

2 cloves garlic, finely chopped

4 teaspoons paprika

1/2 teaspoon salt

1/8 teaspoon pepper

1 cup sour cream

1/4 cup milk

2 teaspoons chopped fresh or 1/4 teaspoon dried dill weed

1/2 cup shredded Cheddar cheese (2 ounces)

1. Cook and drain noodles as directed on package.

2. While noodles are cooking, melt margarine in 10-inch nonstick skillet over medium heat. Cook mushrooms, garlic, paprika, salt and pepper in margarine, stirring occasionally, until mushrooms are tender and most of liquid has evaporated.

3. Mix sour cream, milk and dill weed. Stir into mushroom mixture; cook until hot. Pour mushroom mixture over noodles. Toss with cheese until noodles are well coated.

1 Serving: Calories 255 (Calories from Fat 125); Fat 14g (Saturated 8g); Cholesterol 60mg; Sodium 300mg; Carbohydrate 25g (Dietary Fiber 2g); Protein 9g.

CHICKEN AND MUSHROOM PAPRIKASH: *Omit 1 package of mushrooms. Cut 2 skinless, boneless chicken breast halves into 3/4-inch pieces. Cook chicken in margarine until no longer pink before cooking mushrooms in step 2. Add mushrooms and seasonings. Continue as directed.*

Rice Noodles with Peanut Sauce

PREP: 15 min

4 SERVINGS

Rice stick noodles are white and translucent and can be found in the Asian section of the supermarket. They have a very delicate flavor and texture, making them perfect for soaking up whatever flavors they're mixed with.

8 ounces uncooked rice stick noodles

1/2 cup creamy peanut butter

2 tablespoons soy sauce

1 teaspoon grated gingerroot

1/2 teaspoon crushed red pepper

1/2 cup vegetable or chicken broth

1/4 pound bean sprouts

1 small red bell pepper, cut into 1/4-inch strips

2 medium green onions, sliced (1/4 cup)

2 tablespoons chopped fresh cilantro, if desired

1. Heat 2 quarts water to boiling. Break noodles in half and pull apart slightly; drop into boiling water. Cook uncovered 1 minute; drain. Rinse with cold water; drain.

2. Beat peanut butter, soy sauce, gingerroot and crushed red pepper in small bowl, using wire whisk, until smooth. Gradually beat in broth.

3. Place noodles in large bowl. Add peanut butter mixture, bean sprouts, bell pepper and onions; toss. Sprinkle with cilantro.

1 Serving: Calories 340 (Calories from Fat 155); Fat 17g (Saturated 4g); Cholesterol 0mg; Sodium 790mg; Carbohydrate 39g (Dietary Fiber 3g); Protein 11g.

Lemon-Couscous Skillet Supper

PREP: 10 min; COOK: 15 min

4 SERVINGS

Fresh lemon peel gives this Mediterranean-inspired dish a refreshingly light flavor. Garnish with sliced ripe olives, fresh parsley and a bit of additional lemon peel if desired.

1 tablespoon olive or vegetable oil

1 large onion, chopped (1 cup)

2 cloves garlic, finely chopped

1 can (14 1/2 ounces) ready-to-serve vegetable broth

1 can (15 to 16 ounces) garbanzo beans, rinsed and drained

1 cup frozen baby lima beans

1/2 teaspoon dried oregano leaves

1/2 teaspoon lemon pepper seasoning salt

1 cup uncooked couscous

2 tablespoons chopped fresh parsley

1 teaspoon grated lemon peel

1. Heat oil in 10-inch skillet over medium-high heat. Cook onion and garlic in oil 3 to 5 minutes, stirring occasionally, until onion is crisp-tender.

2. Stir in broth, garbanzo beans, lima beans, oregano and seasoning salt. Heat to boiling; reduce heat to low. Cover and simmer about 5 minutes or until lima beans are tender; remove from heat.

3. Stir in couscous, parsley and lemon peel. Cover and let stand 5 minutes or until liquid is absorbed. Fluff couscous mixture with fork.

1 Serving: Calories 380 (Calories from Fat 55); Fat 6g (Saturated 1g); Cholesterol 0mg; Sodium 730mg; Carbohydrate 75g (Dietary Fiber 11g); Protein 17g.

LEMON-SHRIMP COUSCOUS SKILLET SUPPER: *Add 1/2 pound cooked peeled deveined shrimp with couscous in step 3. Continue as directed.*

Easy Italian Skillet Supper

PREP: 5 min; COOK: 20 min

4 SERVINGS

This is the perfect dish for kids to make for the family supper. It is easy and requires no chopping or cutting if they select to omit the parsley. Try other cheese for a topping, such as Romano, mozzarella, fontina or even Asiago.

1 can (14 1/2 ounces) ready-to-serve vegetable broth

1 1/4 cups uncooked rosamarina (orzo) pasta (8 ounces)

1 can (14 1/2 ounces) diced tomatoes with basil, garlic and oregano, undrained

1 can (15 ounces) black beans, rinsed and drained

2 cups frozen broccoli, cauliflower and carrots (from 16-ounce package)

2 tablespoons chopped fresh parsley, if desired

2 tablespoons shredded Parmesan cheese

1. Heat broth to boiling in 10-inch skillet. Stir in pasta. Heat to boiling; reduce heat to low. Cover and simmer 10 to 12 minutes or until liquid is absorbed.

2. Stir in tomatoes, beans and vegetables. Cover and cook over medium heat 5 to 10 minutes, stirring occasionally, until vegetables are tender.

3. Stir in parsley; sprinkle with cheese.

1 Serving: Calories 305 (Calories from Fat 20); Fat 2g (Saturated 1g); Cholesterol 2mg; Sodium 890mg; Carbohydrate 66g (Dietary Fiber 11g); Protein 17g.

EASY ITALIAN TURKEY SAUSAGE SKILLET SUPPER: *Add 1/2 pound fully cooked smoked turkey sausage link, cut into 1/4-inch slices, with vegetables in step 2. Continue as directed.*

Easy Italian Skillet Supper and Italian Barley and Bean Pilaf (page 164)

Southwest Cheese 'n' Macaroni

PREP: 5 min; COOK: 17 min

6 SERVINGS

If you're on the lookout for recipes to please teenagers and younger children who don't eat meat, give this newfangled version of mac-and-cheese a whirl.

1 1/2 cups milk

1 cup green salsa

1 can (15 ounces) cream-style corn

1 can (11 ounces) whole kernel corn with red and green peppers, drained

1 package (7 ounces) elbow macaroni

8 ounces process cheese product loaf, cubed

1. Mix all ingredients except cheese in 12-inch nonstick skillet. Heat to boiling, stirring occasionally; reduce heat to low. Cover and cook 10 to 14 minutes, stirring frequently, until macaroni is tender.

2. Add cheese; stir until melted.

1 Serving: Calories 405 (Calories from Fat 135); Fat 15g (Saturated 9g); Cholesterol 40mg; Sodium 1060mg; Carbohydrate 53g (Dietary Fiber 4g); Protein 18g.

Mostaccioli with Sun-Dried Tomato Pesto

PREP: 5 min; COOK: 14 min

5 SERVINGS

Keeping an extra batch of sun-dried tomato pesto on hand can be a real lifesaver! That extra batch in the refrigerator or freezer can be tossed with pasta or cooked vegetables and spread on breads or pizza crust.

3 cups uncooked mostaccioli pasta (9 ounces)

Sun-Dried Tomato Pesto (right)

1/2 cup feta cheese, crumbled (4 ounces)

1. Cook and drain pasta as directed on package.

2. While pasta is cooking, prepare Sun-Dried Tomato Pesto. Toss pasta, pesto and cheese.

SUN-DRIED TOMATO PESTO

1/3 cup oil-packed sun-dried tomatoes, drained

1/4 cup firmly packed fresh mint leaves or 4 teaspoons dried mint leaves

2 tablespoons chopped walnuts

2 tablespoons tomato paste

1 tablespoon olive or vegetable oil

1 teaspoon lemon juice

1/2 teaspoon pepper

1 clove garlic

Place all ingredients in food processor or blender. Cover and process until mixture is almost smooth.

1 Serving: Calories 245 (Calories from Fat 70); Fat 8g (Saturated 3g); Cholesterol 10mg; Sodium 200mg; Carbohydrate 37g (Dietary Fiber 2g); Protein 8g.

Mostaccioli Alfredo with Toasted Walnuts

PREP: 3 min; COOK: 17 min

4 SERVINGS

Spread remaining pesto on toasted slices of French bread, then sprinkle with freshly shredded Parmesan cheese. Just before serving, heat in the oven to melt the cheese.

3 cups uncooked mostaccioli pasta (9 ounces)

1 container (10 ounces) refrigerated Alfredo sauce

1/3 cup refrigerated pesto with sun-dried tomatoes (from 7-ounce container)

1/4 cup chopped walnuts, toasted (page 18)

2 tablespoons shredded Parmesan cheese

1. Cook and drain pasta as directed on package; keep warm.

2. Mix Alfredo sauce and pesto in same saucepan. Heat over medium heat, stirring occasionally, until hot.

3. Serve sauce over mostaccioli. Sprinkle with walnuts and cheese.

1 Serving: Calories 615 (Calories from Fat 350); Fat 39g (Saturated 18g); Cholesterol 75mg; Sodium 520mg; Carbohydrate 51g (Dietary Fiber 2g); Protein 17g.

Penne with Radicchio

PREP: 10 min; COOK: 20 min

6 SERVINGS

The key flavor ingredient in this rich dish is the radicchio, a slightly bitter, red-leafed Italian chicory. If radicchio isn't available in your supermarket, use 1 cup of 1/4-inch strips of red cabbage.

4 cups uncooked penne pasta (14 ounces)

2 tablespoons olive or vegetable oil

2 tablespoons margarine or butter

1 medium onion, thinly sliced

1 head radicchio, cut into 1/4-inch strips

1/2 cup dry white wine or vegetable broth

1 cup half-and-half

1/2 teaspoon pepper

1/4 cup freshly grated Parmesan cheese

1. Cook and drain pasta as directed on package.

2. While pasta is cooking, heat oil and margarine in 10-inch skillet over medium-high heat. Cook onion in oil mixture, stirring occasionally until tender. Stir in radicchio; cook until tender. Stir in wine; cook uncovered until liquid has evaporated.

3. Stir in half-and-half and pepper. Heat to boiling; reduce heat. Simmer uncovered about 10 minutes, stirring frequently, until slightly thickened.

4. Mix pasta and radicchio mixture. Sprinkle with cheese.

1 Serving: Calories 490 (Calories from Fat 145); Fat 16g (Saturated 6g); Cholesterol 20mg; Sodium 140mg; Carbohydrate 76g (Dietary Fiber 5g); Protein 15g.

Texas Rotini, Beans and Corn Skillet

PREP: 10 min; COOK: 25 min

6 SERVINGS

The pasta cooks while you prepare the sauce! For a flavor boost, add one to two tablespoons chopped fresh cilantro during the last minute of cooking time.

2 cups uncooked rotini pasta (6 ounces)

1 large onion, chopped (1 cup)

1 medium green bell pepper, chopped (1 cup)

1 can (14 1/2 ounces) Southwestern salsa-style diced tomatoes with green chilies, undrained

1 can (8 ounces) tomato sauce

2 teaspoons chili powder

1/2 teaspoon ground cumin

1/4 teaspoon salt

1 can (15 to 16 ounces) pinto beans, rinsed and drained

1 cup frozen whole kernel corn

1/4 cup shredded Cheddar cheese (1 ounce)

1. Cook and drain pasta as directed on package.

2. While pasta is cooking, spray 10-inch skillet with cooking spray; heat over medium-high heat. Cook onion and bell pepper in skillet 3 to 5 minutes, stirring occasionally, until crisp-tender.

3. Stir in tomatoes, tomato sauce, chili powder, cumin and salt. Cook over medium heat 5 minutes, stirring occasionally.

4. Stir in beans and corn. Cook 5 to 8 minutes, stirring occasionally, until corn is tender.

5. Stir in pasta. Cook, stirring occasionally, until hot. Sprinkle with cheese.

1 Serving: Calories 300 (Calories from Fat 25); Fat 3g (Saturated 2g); Cholesterol 5mg; Sodium 630mg; Carbohydrate 64g (Dietary Fiber 10g); Protein 14g.

TEXAS ROTINI, BEANS AND TURKEY SKILLET: *Add 1/2 pound ground turkey with the onion and bell pepper in step 2. Cook until turkey is no longer pink; drain, if desired. Continue as directed.*

Lemon-Pepper Pasta and Asparagus

PREP: 10 min; COOK: 15 min

4 SERVINGS

Fresh asparagus is now available year-round in most produce departments, so this light and refreshing recipe can be enjoyed more often. For a flavor twist, try fresh lime peel and juice instead of the lemon.

2 cups uncooked farfalle (bow-tie) pasta (4 ounces)

1/4 cup olive or vegetable oil

1 medium red bell pepper, chopped (1 cup)

1 pound asparagus, cut into 1-inch pieces

1 teaspoon grated lemon peel

1/2 teaspoon salt

1/2 teaspoon freshly ground pepper

3 tablespoons lemon juice

1 can (15 to 16 ounces) navy beans, rinsed and drained

Freshly ground pepper

1. Cook and drain pasta as directed on package.

2. While pasta is cooking, heat oil in 12-inch skillet over medium-high heat. Cook bell pepper, asparagus, lemon peel, salt and 1/2 teaspoon pepper in oil, stirring occasionally, until vegetables are crisp-tender.

3. Stir in lemon juice and beans. Cook until beans are hot. Add pasta; toss with vegetable mixture. Sprinkle with pepper.

1 Serving: Calories 360 (Calories from Fat 135); Fat 15g (Saturated 3g); Cholesterol 0mg; Sodium 520mg; Carbohydrate 52g (Dietary Fiber 9g); Protein 13g.

> LEMON-PEPPER PASTA AND SHRIMP: *Add 1/2 pound cooked peeled deveined shrimp with beans in step 3. Continue as directed.*

Lemon-Pepper Pasta and Asparagus

Curried Ravioli with Spinach

PREP: 8 min; COOK: 12 min

4 SERVINGS

Coconut milk is the richly flavored, slightly sweet milk derived from simmering fresh coconut meat and water. It is used extensively in Indonesian cooking. Don't buy cream of coconut by mistake; it's used in making tropical-flavored drinks or desserts.

1 package (9 ounces) refrigerated cheese-filled ravioli

1 package (10 ounces) frozen chopped spinach

1/4 cup cream cheese (2 ounces), softened

2/3 cup canned coconut milk

1/3 cup vegetable or chicken broth

3/4 teaspoon curry powder

1/4 teaspoon salt

3 medium green onions, sliced (1/3 cup)

1/4 cup chopped peanuts

1. Cook and drain ravioli as directed on package. Cook and drain spinach as directed on package.

2. Mix cream cheese, coconut milk, broth, curry powder and salt in 1-quart saucepan. Cook over medium heat, stirring occasionally, until hot.

3. Spoon spinach onto serving plate. Top with ravioli and sauce. Sprinkle with onions and peanuts.

1 Serving: Calories 305 (Calories from Fat 190); Fat 21g (Saturated 12g); Cholesterol 80mg; Sodium 830mg; Carbohydrate 20g (Dietary Fiber 4g); Protein 13g.

Risotto Florentine

PREP: 8 min; COOK: 25 min; STAND: 5 min

4 SERVINGS

Short-grain regular white rice can be used as a substitute for Arborio rice, but the finished dish will be less creamy with more separate, distinct rice grains. The reason? Regular white rice doesn't contain as much starch as Arborio rice.

1 tablespoon margarine or butter

1 medium onion, chopped (1/2 cup)

1 clove garlic, finely chopped

1 cup uncooked Arborio or other
  short-grain white rice

3 cups vegetable broth, heated

1/2 teaspoon saffron threads or
  1/4 teaspoon ground turmeric

1 can (15 to 16 ounces) cannellini beans,
  rinsed and drained

1 package (10 ounces) frozen chopped
  spinach, thawed and squeezed to drain

1/4 cup grated Parmesan cheese

1. Melt margarine in 10-inch skillet over medium-high heat. Cook onion and garlic in margarine, stirring frequently, until onion is crisp-tender.

2. Stir in rice. Cook, stirring frequently, until rice begins to brown.

3. Pour 1/2 cup of the hot broth and the saffron over rice mixture. Cook uncovered over medium heat, stirring frequently, until liquid is absorbed. Continue cooking 15 to 20 minutes, adding broth 1/2 cup at a time and stirring frequently, until rice is almost tender and creamy; remove from heat.

4. Stir in beans and spinach. Sprinkle with cheese. Cover and let stand 5 minutes.

1 Serving: Calories 365 (Calories from Fat 45); Fat 5g (Saturated 2g); Cholesterol 5mg; Sodium 1130mg; Carbohydrate 71g (Dietary Fiber 8g); Protein 17g.

SHRIMP RISOTTO FLORENTINE: *Add 1 can (4 1/2 ounces) medium shrimp, drained and rinsed, with the spinach. Continue as directed.*

Mediterranean Risotto

PREP: 10 min; COOK: 25 min

6 SERVINGS

Broccoli is added at the last minute in this recipe to retain its color, flavor and nutrients. Its crisp-tender texture goes nicely with the creamy richness of the rice. If you don't have feta cheese on hand, sprinkle the risotto with shredded Parmesan cheese.

4 3/4 cups vegetable or chicken broth

4 cloves garlic, finely chopped

1 1/2 cups uncooked Arborio or other short-grain white rice

2 cups broccoli flowerets

1/2 cup oil-packed sun-dried tomatoes, drained and chopped

3/4 cup crumbled feta cheese

1 teaspoon dried oregano leaves

1 can (2 1/4 ounces) sliced ripe olives, drained

1. Heat 1/4 cup of the broth and the garlic to boiling in 12-inch nonstick skillet over medium-high heat. Stir in rice. Cook 1 minute, stirring constantly.

2. Pour 1/2 cup of the broth over rice mixture. Cook uncovered over medium heat, stirring occasionally, until liquid is absorbed. Continue cooking 15 to 20 minutes, adding broth 1/2 cup at a time and stirring occasionally, until rice is almost tender and creamy.

3. Stir in remaining ingredients. Cook 1 minute.

1 Serving: Calories 280 (Calories from Fat 65); Fat 7g (Saturated 4g); Cholesterol 15mg; Sodium 1100mg; Carbohydrate 48g (Dietary Fiber 2g); Protein 8g.

Risotto Primavera

PREP: 10 min; COOK: 25 min

4 SERVINGS

Risottos are very easy to make and will stick to your ribs. To create authentic taste and texture, use Arborio rice, a short-grain rice with a high starch content that lends risotto its creaminess. Add the hot broth a half cup at a time and don't add more until the liquid has been absorbed. This will ensure a wonderful creamy rice dish.

2 teaspoons olive or vegetable oil

1 medium onion, chopped (1/2 cup)

1 small carrot, cut into julienne strips

1 cup uncooked Arborio or other short-grain white rice

2 cans (14 1/2 ounces each) ready-to-serve vegetable broth, heated

1 cup broccoli flowerets

1 cup frozen green peas

1 small zucchini, cut into julienne strips

2 tablespoons grated Parmesan cheese

1. Heat oil in 3-quart nonstick saucepan over medium-high heat. Cook onion and carrot in oil, stirring frequently, until crisp-tender.

2. Stir in rice. Cook, stirring frequently, until rice begins to brown.

3. Pour 1/2 cup of the hot broth over rice mixture. Cook uncovered over medium heat, stirring frequently, until liquid is absorbed. Continue cooking 15 to 20 minutes, adding broth 1/2 cup at a time and stirring frequently, until rice is almost tender and creamy. Add broccoli, peas and zucchini with the last addition of broth. Sprinkle with cheese.

1 Serving: Calories 265 (Calories from Fat 35); Fat 4g (Saturated 1g); Cholesterol 2mg; Sodium 950mg; Carbohydrate 53g (Dietary Fiber 4g); Protein 8g.

Sweet Potato Risotto

PREP: 8 min; COOK: 25 min

4 SERVINGS

Learn to love sweet potatoes! These deep, orange-colored tubers are full of vitamins A and C. You can use either mashed fresh cooked or canned sweet potatoes. For another golden treat, use mashed cooked carrots instead of sweet potatoes.

2 tablespoons dry white wine or water

1/3 cup chopped onion

1 clove garlic, finely chopped

**1 cup uncooked Arborio or other
    short-grain white rice**

1/2 cup mashed cooked sweet potato

**3 3/4 cups vegetable or chicken broth,
    heated**

2 tablespoons grated Parmesan cheese

**1/2 teaspoon chopped fresh or 1/4 teaspoon
    dried rosemary leaves, crumbled**

1/8 teaspoon ground nutmeg

Shredded Parmesan cheese, if desired

1. Spray 3-quart nonstick saucepan with cooking spray. Heat wine to boiling in saucepan over medium-high heat. Cook onion and garlic in wine 3 to 4 minutes, stirring frequently, until onion is tender.

2. Stir in rice. Cook 1 minute, stirring frequently, until rice begins to brown.

3. Stir in sweet potato and 1/2 cup of the broth. Cook uncovered over medium heat, stirring frequently, until liquid is absorbed. Continue cooking 15 to 20 minutes, adding broth 1/2 cup at a time and stirring frequently, until rice is almost tender and creamy; remove from heat. Stir in remaining ingredients. Garnish with additional fresh rosemary and shredded Parmesan cheese.

1 Serving: Calories 260 (Calories from Fat 25); Fat 3g (Saturated 1g); Cholesterol 2mg; Sodium 1030mg; Carbohydrate 50g (Dietary Fiber 2g); Protein 10g.

"Fried" Wild Rice with Corn

Prep: 10 min; Cook: 11 min

4 Servings

Fried rice doesn't have to have pork, shrimp, egg or even white rice in it to taste great. Don't believe it? For a real kick, try this nutty-flavored, corn- and carrot-spiked version! If wild rice isn't on your pantry shelf use cooked white or brown rice.

1/2 cup vegetable or chicken broth

8 medium green onions, chopped (1/2 cup)

2 cloves garlic, finely chopped

1/2 cup sliced mushrooms (1 1/2 ounces)

1/4 cup shredded carrot

1 cup frozen whole kernel corn

3 cups cooked wild rice

1 tablespoon soy sauce

1/8 teaspoon pepper

Chopped green onion, if desired

1. Heat broth to boiling in 10-inch nonstick skillet over medium-high heat. Cook 1/2 cup onions, the garlic, mushrooms and carrot in broth 5 to 8 minutes, stirring frequently, until vegetables are crisp-tender.

2. Stir in corn and wild rice. Cook 3 minutes, stirring constantly (mixture will be dry).

3. Stir in soy sauce and pepper; cook until hot. Sprinkle with onion.

1 Serving: Calories 175 (Calories from Fat 10); Fat 1g (Saturated 0g); Cholesterol 0mg; Sodium 390mg; Carbohydrate 39g (Dietary Fiber 4g); Protein 7g.

"FRIED" WILD RICE WITH CHICKEN: *Decrease wild rice to 2 cups. Add 1 cup finely chopped cooked chicken or turkey with the wild rice in step 2. Continue as directed.*

Vegetable-Rice Skillet

PREP: 5 min; COOK: 9 min

4 SERVINGS

This recipe meets the requirements for today's cooking style of "assembling" ingredients—one can, one box and one bag—for a delicious meal in minutes.

1 can (14 1/2 ounces) ready-to-serve vegetable broth

2 tablespoons margarine or butter

1 package (16 ounces) frozen cauliflower, carrots and asparagus

1 package (6.2 ounces) long grain and wild rice fast-cooking mix

3/4 cup shredded Cheddar cheese (3 ounces)

1. Heat broth and margarine to boiling in 10-inch skillet. Stir in vegetables, rice and contents of seasoning packet. Heat to boiling; reduce heat.

2. Cover and simmer 5 to 6 minutes or until vegetables and rice are tender. Sprinkle with cheese.

1 Serving: Calories 215 (Calories from Fat 115); Fat 13g (Saturated 6g); Cholesterol 25mg; Sodium 810mg; Carbohydrate 18g (Dietary Fiber 3g); Protein 9g.

Fiesta Rice and Vermicelli

PREP: 3 min; COOK: 25 min

6 SERVINGS

2 tablespoons margarine or butter

1 package (6.8 ounces) rice and vermicelli mix with Spanish seasonings

2 cups water

1 teaspoon chili powder

1 jar (16 ounces) thick-and-chunky salsa

1 package (16 ounces) frozen corn, broccoli and red peppers

1 can (15 to 16 ounces) pinto beans, rinsed and drained

1 cup shredded Cheddar cheese (4 ounces)

1. Melt margarine in 12-inch nonstick skillet over medium heat. Stir in rice and vermicelli mix. Cook, stirring constantly, until golden brown.

2. Stir in contents of seasoning packet, water, chili powder and salsa. Heat to boiling; reduce heat to low. Cover and simmer 15 to 20 minutes, stirring occasionally, until rice is tender.

3. Stir in vegetables and beans. Cook until hot. Sprinkle with cheese.

1 Serving: Calories 265 (Calories from Fat 100); Fat 11g (Saturated 5g); Cholesterol 20mg; Sodium 720mg; Carbohydrate 38g (Dietary Fiber 10g); Protein 14g.

TURKEY FIESTA RICE AND VERMICELLI: *Add 1/2 pound ground turkey with rice and vermicelli mix in step 1. Cook until no longer pink; drain if desired. Continue as directed.*

Asian Rice and Lentil Patties

PREP: 20 min; COOK: 50 min

4 SERVINGS

Stir-fry sauce is available in many flavor variations from sweet-and-sour to teriyaki. Use your favorite to make this nutritious supper dish. If you don't have stir-fry sauce, try bottled sweet-and-sour sauce instead.

1/2 cup uncooked brown rice

1/4 cup dried lentils (2 ounces), sorted and rinsed

1 1/2 cups water

1/4 cup finely chopped cashews

2 tablespoons dry bread crumbs

2 tablespoons stir-fry sauce

4 medium green onions, finely chopped (1/2 cup)

1 egg, beaten

Vegetable Sauce (right)

Hot cooked Chinese noodles or rice, if desired

1. Heat rice, lentils and water to boiling in 2-quart saucepan; reduce heat to low. Cover and simmer 30 to 40 minutes, stirring occasionally, until lentils are tender and water is absorbed. Cool slightly.

2. Mash rice mixture slightly with fork. Stir in remaining ingredients except Vegetable Sauce. Shape mixture into 4 patties, each about 1/2 inch thick.

3. Spray 10-inch skillet with cooking spray. Cook patties in skillet about 10 minutes, turning once, until golden brown. Remove patties from skillet; keep warm.

4. Prepare Vegetable Sauce in same skillet. Add patties. Cover and cook over medium heat 5 to 8 minutes or until patties are hot. Serve sauce and patties over Chinese noodles or rice.

VEGETABLE SAUCE

1 medium stalk celery, sliced (1/2 cup)

1 medium carrot, sliced (1/2 cup)

1/2 cup water

2 tablespoons stir-fry sauce

Heat all ingredients to boiling; reduce heat to medium. Cover and cook about 5 minutes, stirring occasionally, until vegetables are crisp-tender.

1 Serving: Calories 210 (Calories from Fat 55); Fat 6g (Saturated 2g); Cholesterol 55mg; Sodium 720mg; Carbohydrate 34g (Dietary Fiber 5g); Protein 10g.

Rio Grande Rice and Beans

PREP: 10 min; COOK: 8 min

4 SERVINGS

For the richest flavor, use a fully ripe avocado that yields to gentle pressure. The Haas variety, characterized by its oval shape and pebbly skin changing from green to black as it ripens, is higher in fat than other varieties, making it rich, buttery and more flavorful.

1 1/3 cups vegetable or chicken broth

1 1/3 cups uncooked instant rice

1/4 teaspoon pepper

1 can (15 to 16 ounces) kidney beans, rinsed and drained

3 medium green onions, sliced (1/3 cup)

1 large avocado, diced

2 teaspoons lime juice

1 medium green onion, sliced (2 tablespoons)

1. Heat broth to boiling in 2-quart saucepan. Stir in rice and pepper; remove from heat. Cover and let steam about 5 minutes or until liquid is absorbed.

2. Fluff rice with fork. Stir in beans and 1/3 cup onions.

3. Mix avocado and lime juice; gently fold into rice. Sprinkle with 2 tablespoons onion.

1 Serving: Calories 280 (Calories from Fat 65); Fat 7g (Saturated 2g); Cholesterol 0mg; Sodium 650mg; Carbohydrate 51g (Dietary Fiber 7g); Protein 10g.

Italian Country Vegetable-Barley Skillet

PREP: 8 min; COOK: 20 min

6 SERVINGS

Flavored oils are becoming more readily available in supermarkets. If you can't find garlic-flavored oil, use two tablespoons vegetable or olive oil and one-half teaspoon garlic powder in place of the flavored oil.

2 tablespoons garlic-flavored oil

2 medium carrots, sliced (1 cup)

1 medium zucchini, sliced (2 cups)

1 large yellow summer squash, sliced (2 cups)

1 package (8 ounces) sliced mushrooms

1/2 medium red onion, cut into wedges

1 cup uncooked quick-cooking barley

1 cup water

1 jar (28 ounces) chunky spaghetti sauce

1 cup shredded Italian-style six-cheese blend (4 ounces)

1. Heat oil in 12-inch nonstick skillet over medium-high heat. Cook carrots, zucchini, squash, mushrooms and onion in oil about 10 minutes, stirring occasionally, until vegetables are tender.

2. Stir in barley, water and spaghetti sauce. Heat to boiling; reduce heat to low. Cook and simmer 10 to 12 minutes, stirring occasionally, until barley is tender; remove from heat. Sprinkle with cheese.

1 Serving: Calories 355 (Calories from Fat 115); Fat 13g (Saturated 4g); Cholesterol 10mg; Sodium 760mg; Carbohydrate 57g (Dietary Fiber 9g); Protein 12g.

Spiced Bulgur-and-Barley Balls

PREP: 15 min; COOK: 12 min

4 SERVINGS

These bulgur-and-barley balls can be used in all the same ways as meatballs. Line them up in a hot dog bun, drizzle with ketchup and mustard and you have a great sandwich. Or top pasta with your favorite sauce and these tasty little grain balls.

2 1/4 cups cooked bulgur

1 1/2 cups cooked barley

1/4 cup milk

2 tablespoons dry bread crumbs

1/2 teaspoon salt

1/4 teaspoon ground nutmeg

1/4 teaspoon ground allspice

1 egg, beaten

1/4 cup ground walnuts

2 tablespoons margarine or butter

1. Mix all ingredients except walnuts and margarine. Shape mixture into 1-inch balls. Roll balls in walnuts.

2. Melt margarine in 10-inch skillet over medium-high heat. Cook balls in margarine 10 to 12 minutes, turning frequently, until light brown.

1 Serving: Calories 255 (Calories from Fat 100); Fat 11g (Saturated 3g); Cholesterol 55mg; Sodium 440mg; Carbohydrate 39g (Dietary Fiber 8g); Protein 8g.

Italian Barley and Bean Pilaf

PREP: 8 min; COOK: 16 min

6 SERVINGS

Regular white mushrooms, cut in half, can be used in place of the portobello mushrooms in this hearty and robust Italian skillet dish. Use regular vegetable or olive oil and half a teaspoon garlic powder in place of the flavored oil.

2 tablespoons garlic-flavored oil

1 large onion, chopped (1 cup)

6 ounces portobello mushrooms, sliced

2 cans (14 1/2 ounces each) diced tomatoes with basil, garlic and oregano, undrained

3/4 cup uncooked quick-cooking barley

1 teaspoon dried thyme leaves

1 can (15 to 19 ounces) cannellini beans, rinsed and drained

3 cups lightly packed spinach leaves, cut into 1/2-inch strips

3/4 cup shredded Parmesan cheese

1. Heat oil in 12-inch nonstick skillet over medium-high heat. Cook onion and mushrooms in oil, stirring frequently, until tender.

2. Stir in tomatoes, barley and thyme; reduce heat to low. Cover and simmer 12 to 15 minutes, stirring occasionally, until barley is tender.

3. Stir in beans, spinach and 1/2 cup of the cheese; cook until hot. Sprinkle with remaining 1/4 cup cheese.

1 Serving: Calories 285 (Calories from Fat 80); Fat 9g (Saturated 3g); Cholesterol 10mg; Sodium 580mg; Carbohydrate 46g (Dietary Fiber 10g); Protein 15g.

Grecian Kasha and Lentils

PREP: 5 min; COOK: 22 min

6 SERVINGS

To find kasha, also called roasted buckwheat kernels or groats, you may need to look in the health, cereal or kosher-food section of your supermarket. If you haven't tried kasha before, we think you will enjoy its toasty, nutty flavor.

1/2 cup uncooked kasha

1 egg white

2 cloves garlic, finely chopped

4 cups vegetable or chicken broth

3/4 cup dried lentils (6 ounces), sorted and rinsed

1 teaspoon ground cumin

1 can (15 1/4 ounces) whole kernel corn, drained

1 can (2 1/4 ounces) sliced ripe olives, drained

2 medium tomatoes, chopped (1 1/2 cups)

1 container (8 ounces) plain yogurt

1 1/2 teaspoons dried mint leaves

1 cup crumbled feta cheese

1. Spray 12-inch nonstick skillet with cooking spray; heat over medium-high heat. Mix kasha and egg white. Cook kasha and garlic in skillet 2 to 3 minutes, stirring constantly, until kernels separate and dry.

2. Stir in broth, lentils and cumin. Heat to boiling; reduce heat to low. Cover and simmer 20 to 25 minutes, stirring occasionally, until kasha and lentils are tender. Stir in corn, olives and tomato. Cook until hot.

3. Mix yogurt and mint. Spoon over kasha mixture. Sprinkle with cheese.

1 Serving: Calories 265 (Calories from Fat 70); Fat 8g (Saturated 5g); Cholesterol 25mg; Sodium 1250mg; Carbohydrate 41g (Dietary Fiber 8g); Protein 15g.

Polenta Primavera

PREP: 15 min; COOK: 20 min

4 SERVINGS

Polenta is available in the refrigerated section of many large supermarkets. For this recipe, you can use plain polenta or try one of the new flavored varieties, such as sun-dried tomato. Fennel seed has a mild anise, or licorice, flavor and is often used in Italian sausage. If you don't care for this flavor, just leave it out and you will still have a tasty dish.

1 tube (16 ounces) refrigerated polenta, cut into 1/2-inch slices

2 tablespoons olive or vegetable oil

1 small red onion, cut into thin wedges

2 cloves garlic, finely chopped

1/2 pound green beans, cut into 3/4-inch pieces

1 medium red bell pepper, coarsely chopped (1 cup)

1 1/2 cup mushrooms, sliced (4 ounces)

1 small yellow summer squash, cut lengthwise in half, then cut crosswise into 1/4-inch slices

1/2 teaspoon fennel seed, crushed

1/4 teaspoon salt

1/4 cup finely shredded mozzarella cheese (1 ounce)

1. Cook polenta as directed on package.

2. While polenta is cooking, heat oil in 10-inch skillet over medium-high heat. Cook onion and garlic in oil 3 to 5 minutes, stirring occasionally, until crisp-tender.

3. Stir in green beans and bell pepper. Cover and cook over medium-low heat 8 to 10 minutes, stirring occasionally, until beans are crisp-tender. Stir in mushrooms, squash, fennel and salt. Cover and cook 3 to 5 minutes, stirring occasionally, until squash is crisp-tender.

4. Serve polenta over vegetable mixture. Sprinkle each serving with cheese.

1 Serving: Calories 210 (Calories from Fat 70); Fat 8g (Saturated 2g); Cholesterol 5mg; Sodium 630mg; Carbohydrate 30g (Dietary Fiber 3g); Protein 7g.

Skillet Cassoulet

PREP: 10 min; COOK: 23 min

4 SERVINGS

A cassoulet is a classic French dish made with white beans and a variety of meats. Traditionally, it is covered and simmered slowly to blend the flavors. We find this quicker version without meat still makes a tasty hearty meal that will satisfy anyone's appetite.

1 tablespoon olive or vegetable oil

2 medium stalks celery, sliced (1 cup)

2 medium carrots, sliced (1 cup)

1 medium onion, chopped (1/2 cup)

1 can (15 to 16 ounces) great northern beans, rinsed and drained

1 can (15 to 16 ounces) dark red kidney beans, rinsed and drained

1 can (14 1/2 ounces) stewed tomatoes, undrained

2 tablespoons molasses

3/4 teaspoon dried thyme leaves

1/4 teaspoon salt

2 tablespoons chopped fresh parsley

1. Heat oil in 12-inch skillet over medium-high heat. Cook celery, carrots and onion in oil 4 to 6 minutes, stirring occasionally, until crisp-tender.

2. Stir in remaining ingredients except parsley. Cook uncovered over medium-low heat 10 to 15 minutes or until vegetables are tender. Sprinkle with parsley.

1 Serving: Calories 285 (Calories from Fat 35); Fat 4g (Saturated 1g); Cholesterol 0mg; Sodium 1040mg; Carbohydrate 59g (Dietary Fiber 13g); Protein 16g.

SKILLET CASSOULET WITH TURKEY SAUSAGE: *Add 1/2 pound fully cooked smoked turkey sausage link, cut into 1/4-inch slices, with remaining ingredients in step 2. Continue as directed.*

Mexicana Mixed Beans with Corn Bread

PREP: 5 min; COOK: 5 min

4 SERVINGS

This recipe is perfect to serve when you need dinner in a hurry. Keep a package of corn muffin mix on hand, or keep store-bought corn muffins in your freezer.

1 cup thick-and-chunky salsa

1 can (15 ounces) black beans, undrained

1 can (15 to 16 ounces) chili beans in sauce, undrained

1 can (15 to 16 ounces) garbanzo beans, rinsed and drained

4 two-inch squares corn bread or corn muffins, warmed

Sour cream, if desired

Chopped fresh cilantro, if desired

1. Mix salsa and beans in 12-inch skillet. Cook over medium-high heat, stirring occasionally, until hot.

2. Serve bean mixture over corn bread. Top with a dollop of sour cream. Sprinkle with cilantro.

1 Serving: Calories 510 (Calories from Fat 90); Fat 10g (Saturated 4g); Cholesterol 45mg; Sodium 1520mg; Carbohydrate 97g (Dietary Fiber 19g); Protein 27g.

Crunchy Bean Skillet

PREP: 8 min; COOK: 10 min

6 SERVINGS

In certain regions of Italy, it is not uncommon to see cannellini beans bathed with a tomato or spaghetti sauce—the flavors get along very well! Great northern beans can be used instead of the cannellini.

3 cans (15 to 16 ounces each) cannellini beans, rinsed and drained

1 jar (14 ounces) spaghetti sauce

2 medium stalks celery, sliced (1 cup)

4 medium green onions, sliced (1/2 cup)

1 tablespoon chopped fresh or 1 teaspoon dried basil leaves

2 teaspoons chopped fresh or 1/2 teaspoon dried oregano leaves

1 cup shredded mozzarella cheese (4 ounces)

1/2 cup coarsely chopped walnuts

2 tablespoons chopped fresh parsley, if desired

1. Mix all ingredients except cheese and walnuts in 10-inch skillet. Heat to boiling; reduce heat.

2. Sprinkle with cheese. Cover and simmer 3 to 5 minutes or just until cheese is melted. Sprinkle with walnuts and parsley.

1 Serving: Calories 270 (Calories from Fat 110); Fat 12g (Saturated 3g); Cholesterol 10mg; Sodium 590mg; Carbohydrate 32g (Dietary Fiber 6g); Protein 14g.

Vegetables Sauté with Black Beans and Couscous

PREP: 10 min; COOK: 8 min

4 SERVINGS

Fennel is an aromatic plant with pale green, celerylike stems and bright green feathery leaves that resemble dill weed. Fennel is sometimes called sweet anise and people associate it with licorice. However, it has a milder and sweeter flavor than anise and the flavor becomes even milder when it is cooked.

1 teaspoon olive or vegetable oil

1 medium red onion, thinly sliced

1 large red bell pepper, cut crosswise in half, then cut lengthwise into thin slices

1 small bulb fennel, cut into fourths and thinly sliced

2 tablespoons chopped fresh or 2 teaspoons dried oregano leaves

1/4 teaspoon crushed red pepper

2 cans (15 ounces each) black beans, rinsed and drained

2 cups hot cooked couscous

1. Heat oil in 10-inch skillet over medium-high heat. Cook onion, bell pepper and fennel in oil 2 to 3 minutes, stirring occasionally, until crisp-tender.

2. Stir in oregano, red pepper and beans; reduce heat. Simmer uncovered 5 minutes. Serve with couscous.

1 Serving: Calories 355 (Calories from Fat 25); Fat 3g (Saturated 1g); Cholesterol 0mg; Sodium 670mg; Carbohydrate 78g (Dietary Fiber 17g); Protein 21g.

Sweet Potatoes and Black Beans

PREP: 10 min; COOK: 15 min

4 SERVINGS

In a hurry? You can skip cooking the fresh sweet potatoes and use vacuum-packed canned sweet potatoes (16-ounce size) cut into 3/4-inch cubes. If you don't have cooked rice on hand, use instant rice or boil-in-the bag rice to have cooked rice in 10 minutes.

3 medium sweet potatoes, peeled and cut into 3/4-inch cubes (3 cups)

3/4 cup orange juice

2 teaspoons cornstarch

1/2 teaspoon ground allspice

1/2 teaspoon ground coriander

1/2 teaspoon grated gingerroot or 1/4 teaspoon ground ginger

1/4 teaspoon ground cumin

1 can (15 ounces) black beans, rinsed and drained

1 cup cooked white rice

1. Place sweet potatoes in 2-quart saucepan; add just enough water to cover. Heat to boiling; reduce heat. Cover and simmer 10 to 12 minutes or until tender; drain and set aside.

2. Mix remaining ingredients except beans and rice in same saucepan. Heat to boiling, stirring constantly. Boil and stir about 1 minute or until thickened.

3. Stir in sweet potatoes, beans and rice. Cook about 2 minutes or until hot.

1 Serving: Calories 270 (Calories from Fat 10); Fat 1g (Saturated 0g); Cholesterol 0mg; Sodium 230mg; Carbohydrate 63g (Dietary Fiber 9g); Protein 11g.

SWEET POTATOES AND BLACK BEANS WITH HAM: *Omit the rice. Add 1 cup cubed fully cooked turkey ham with the beans in step 3. Continue as directed.*

Butter Bean Patties with Southwestern Sauce

PREP: 15 min; COOK: 18 min

4 SERVINGS

To make mashing the beans easier, use a food processor or potato masher. If you don't have chili sauce or cumin, use ketchup and dried oregano leaves instead. For a Southwest cheeseburger, top each patty with a slice of American cheese after turning and serve in a hamburger bun topped with the Southwest sauce.

1 can (15 to 16 ounces) butter beans, rinsed and drained

10 round buttery crackers, crushed (1/3 cup)

1 egg, beaten

2 tablespoons chili sauce

2 tablespoons finely chopped onion

Southwestern Sauce (right)

1. Mash beans in medium bowl. Stir in crackers, egg, chili sauce and onion. Shape mixture into 4 patties, each about 1/2 inch thick.

2. Spray 10-inch skillet with cooking spray. Cook patties in skillet 8 to 10 minutes, turning once, until golden brown. Remove from skillet; keep warm.

3. Add all Southwestern Sauce ingredients to skillet. Cook over medium-low heat 5 to 8 minutes, stirring occasionally, until vegetables are tender. Serve sauce over patties.

SOUTHWESTERN SAUCE

1 cup frozen mixed vegetables

1/4 cup raisins

1/4 teaspoon ground cumin

1 can (14 1/2 ounces) Mexican-style stewed tomatoes with jalapeños and spices, undrained

1 Serving: Calories 230 (Calories from Fat 35); Fat 4g (Saturated 1g); Cholesterol 55mg; Sodium 700mg; Carbohydrate 47g (Dietary Fiber 10g); Protein 12g.

Butter Bean Patties with Southwestern Sauce

Spicy Garbanzos

PREP: 8 min; COOK: 8 min

4 SERVINGS

Mustard seeds, available in both white and brown varieties, add unexpected flavor and crunch to food.

1 tablespoon vegetable oil

1 teaspoon mustard seed

1 large onion, chopped (1 cup)

1/2 cup vegetable or chicken broth

2 tablespoons tomato paste

1/2 teaspoon salt

1/4 teaspoon ground cinnamon

1/8 teaspoon ground cloves

2 cans (15 to 16 ounces each) garbanzo beans, rinsed and drained

2 tablespoons chopped parsley, if desired

1. Heat oil in 2-quart saucepan over medium-high heat. Cook mustard seed and onion in oil, stirring occasionally, until onion is tender.

2. Stir in remaining ingredients. Cook about 5 minutes, stirring occasionally, until beans are hot. Sprinkle with parsley.

1 Serving: Calories 270 (Calories from Fat 70); Fat 8g (Saturated 1g); Cholesterol 0mg; Sodium 830mg; Carbohydrate 45g (Dietary Fiber 9g); Protein 14g.

Italian Bean Cakes

PREP: 10 min; COOK: 10 min

6 SERVINGS

Bean patties are more delicate than ground beef patties, so hold down your exuberance when turning them over with a spatula—use a gentle touch. These bean patties make great California burgers. Serve on hamburger buns topped with slices of raw onion, lettuce, juicy tomato slices and mayonnaise.

2 cans (15 to 16 ounces each) great northern or cannellini beans, rinsed and drained

1/2 cup dry Italian seasoned bread crumbs

1/4 cup chopped fresh or 1 teaspoon dried basil leaves

3/4 teaspoon garlic salt

1 egg, beaten

2 tablespoons olive or vegetable oil

Hot spaghetti sauce, if desired

1. Mash beans in large bowl. Stir in remaining ingredients. Shape into 6 patties, each about 1/2 inch thick.

2. Heat oil in 12-inch nonstick skillet over medium heat. Cook patties in skillet 8 to 10 minutes, turning once, until golden brown.

3. Serve with spaghetti sauce.

1 Serving: Calories 230 (Calories from Fat 55); Fat 6g (Saturated 1g); Cholesterol 35mg; Sodium 510mg; Carbohydrate 38g (Dietary Fiber 8g); Protein 14g.

Unleaded Beans

Flatulence, commonly known as intestinal gas, can result from eating beans. Gas is caused by the digestive system's inability to digest the complex sugars found in beans.

You can reduce this effect by draining the soaking liquid used to hydrate dried beans before cooking or by rinsing and draining canned beans. In case you were wondering, minimal nutrition is lost by draining dried or canned beans.

You may also want to check out the over-the-counter products available in liquid and tablet form to help minimize gas.

When adding more beans to your diet, add them gradually over a period of several weeks to allow your digestive system time to adjust. Sudden consumption of large amounts of beans can cause bloating and gas.

5

One-Dish Oven Meals

Alfredo Pasta Pie with
Toasted French Bread Crust
(page 204)

Onion and Cheese Pie

PREP: 20 min; BAKE: 45 min

6 SERVINGS

Quickly and easily crush crackers into crumbs by sealing them in a plastic bag and pounding with your hand. Fresh juicy tomatoes from the garden or farmer's market cut into thick slices are perfect with this warm cheese dish.

1 1/4 cups finely crushed saltine crackers (36 squares)

1/4 cup margarine or butter, melted

2 tablespoons margarine or butter

2 large onions, chopped (2 cups)

1 1/2 cups shredded sharp Cheddar cheese (6 ounces)

1 cup milk

1/2 teaspoon salt

1/4 teaspoon pepper

3 eggs

1. Heat oven to 325°. Grease pie plate, 9 × 1 1/4 inches. Mix cracker crumbs and 1/4 cup melted margarine; press evenly in bottom and up side of pie plate.

2. Melt 2 tablespoons margarine in 10-inch skillet over medium-high heat. Cook onions in margarine 5 to 6 minutes, stirring frequently, until light brown. Spread onions in crust. Sprinkle with cheese.

3. Beat milk, salt, pepper and eggs until blended; pour over cheese.

4. Bake uncovered 40 to 45 minutes or until knife inserted in center comes out clean. Serve immediately.

1 Serving: Calories 370 (Calories from Fat 245); Fat 27g (Saturated 10g); Cholesterol 140mg; Sodium 740mg; Carbohydrate 19g (Dietary Fiber 1g); Protein 14g.

Cheesy Vegetable Strata

PREP: 15 min; CHILL: 2 hr; BAKE: 1 hr 15 min; STAND: 10 min

8 SERVINGS

For a lighter version of this recipe, use 2 cups reduced-fat shredded Cheddar cheese for regular, 2 cups fat-free cholesterol-free egg substitute for the 8 eggs and 4 cups skim milk instead of whole milk.

8 slices bread

1 package (16 ounces) frozen broccoli, green beans, pearl onions and red peppers, thawed and drained

2 cups shredded sharp Cheddar cheese (8 ounces)

8 eggs, slightly beaten

4 cups milk

1 teaspoon salt

1 teaspoon ground mustard (dry)

1/4 teaspoon pepper

1/4 teaspoon ground red pepper (cayenne)

1. Cut each bread slice diagonally into 4 triangles. Arrange half of the bread in ungreased rectangular pan, 13 × 9 × 2 inches. Top with vegetables. Sprinkle with cheese. Top with remaining bread.

2. Beat remaining ingredients until blended; pour over bread. Cover and refrigerate at least 2 hours but no longer than 24 hours.

3. Heat oven to 325°. Cover and bake 30 minutes. Uncover and bake about 45 minutes longer or until knife inserted in center comes out clean. Let stand 10 minutes before cutting.

1 Serving: Calories 325 (Calories from Fat 160); Fat 18g (Saturated 10g); Cholesterol 250mg; Sodium 730mg; Carbohydrate 23g (Dietary Fiber 2g); Protein 20g.

CHEESY VEGETABLE-HAM STRATA: *Sprinkle 1 cup chopped fully cooked smoked turkey ham over the vegetables in step 2. Reduce salt to 1/2 teaspoon. Continue as directed.*

Creamy Herbed Vegetables

PREP: 15 min; BAKE: 25 min

4 SERVINGS

Use any sixteen-ounce package of mixed vegetables for this creamy dish. The crushed crackers on top make an easy and tasty crunchy topping—a cup of corn flake cereal also makes a good topping.

1 package (16 ounces) frozen broccoli, carrots and cauliflower

2 tablespoons margarine or butter

2 tablespoons all-purpose flour

1/4 cup milk

1 1/2 cups small curd creamed cottage cheese

1 tablespoon chopped fresh or 1 teaspoon dried marjoram leaves

1/4 teaspoon salt

1/4 teaspoon pepper

1 cup coarsely crushed round buttery crackers (about 20 crackers)

1. Heat oven to 375°. Grease square pan, 8 × 8 × 2 inches.

2. Cook vegetables in saucepan as directed on package; drain. Spread vegetables in pan.

3. Melt margarine in same saucepan over medium heat. Stir in flour. Gradually stir in milk. Heat to boiling, stirring constantly; remove from heat. Stir in cottage cheese, marjoram, salt and pepper. Spread sauce over vegetables. Sprinkle with cracker crumbs.

4. Bake uncovered 20 to 25 minutes or until bubbly around edges and crumbs are light brown.

1 Serving: Calories 260 (Calories from Fat 125); Fat 14g (Saturated 5g); Cholesterol 15mg; Sodium 850mg; Carbohydrate 22g (Dietary Fiber 3g); Protein 14g.

CREAMY HERBED CHICKEN AND VEGETABLES: *Add 2 cups cubed cooked chicken or turkey with cottage cheese in step 3. Continue as directed.*

Baked Asparagus and Couscous

PREP: 10 min; BAKE: 30 min

6 SERVINGS

Here's a quick and easy casserole with lots of flavor and color. Use any flavor of cream soup you have on hand. Break off tough ends of asparagus by breaking off the stalk as far down as it snaps easily. This is a fast and sure way of removing any of the stalk that isn't tender.

1 1/4 cups vegetable or chicken broth,
    heated

1 pound asparagus, cut into 2-inch pieces

1 cup uncooked couscous

1 can (10 3/4 ounces) condensed cream of
    asparagus soup

2 medium carrots, shredded (1 1/2 cups)

1 tablespoon lemon juice

1 teaspoon fresh or 1/2 teaspoon dried
    dill weed

1/2 teaspoon salt

1 cup soft bread crumbs (about
    1 1/2 slices bread)

2 tablespoons margarine or butter, melted

1. Heat oven to 425°.

2. Mix broth, asparagus, couscous, soup, carrots, lemon juice, dill weed and salt in 2-quart casserole. Cover and bake 20 minutes or until hot and bubbly.

3. Toss bread crumbs and margarine; sprinkle over asparagus mixture. Bake uncovered 8 to 10 minutes or until crumbs are golden brown.

1 Serving: Calories 270 (Calories from Fat 70); Fat 8g (Saturated 2g); Cholesterol 2mg; Sodium 990mg; Carbohydrate 46g (Dietary Fiber 4g); Protein 8g

> BAKED ASPARAGUS, HAM AND COUSCOUS:
> *Add 1 cup cubed fully cooked smoked turkey ham with asparagus in step 2. Continue as directed.*

Cabbage and Rice Pie with Herbed Tomato Sauce

PREP: 20 min; BAKE: 25 min

6 SERVINGS

Puff pastry is made of hundreds of layers of chilled butter and pastry dough. As it bakes, the moisture in the butter creates steam, causing the dough to puff and separate into hundreds of flaky layers. The golden flaky layers are the perfect texture contrast for the creamy vegetable filling.

1 1/2 cups water

1 teaspoon salt

1/4 teaspoon pepper

3 cups shredded green cabbage

2 cups refrigerated or frozen shredded hash brown potatoes

1 1/4 cups uncooked instant rice

1 package (8 ounces) cream cheese, softened

1 tablespoon chopped fresh or 1 teaspoon dried sage leaves

1/2 package (17 1/4-ounce size) frozen puff pastry (1 sheet), thawed

1 can (10 3/4 ounces) condensed tomato with herbs soup

1/4 cup water

1. Heat oven to 400°. Grease deep-dish pie plate, 9 × 1 1/2 inches.

2. Heat 1 1/2 cups water to boiling in 3-quart saucepan. Stir in salt, pepper, cabbage and potatoes. Heat to boiling; reduce heat to medium. Cover and cook 5 minutes.

3. Stir in rice, cream cheese and sage; remove from heat. Cover and let stand 5 minutes. Stir cabbage mixture; spoon into pie plate.

4. Unfold pastry sheet; place over cabbage mixture. Trim pastry to fit pie plate. Press edge of pastry onto edge of pie plate, using fork.

5. Bake uncovered about 25 minutes or until golden brown. During last 5 minutes of baking, heat soup and 1/4 cup water in 1-quart saucepan over medium-low heat. Serve pie with sauce.

1 Serving: Calories 300 (Calories from Fat 135); Fat 15g (Saturated 9g); Cholesterol 40mg; Sodium 820mg; Carbohydrate 37g (Dietary Fiber 2g); Protein 6g.

Eggplant and Gouda Cheese Pie

PREP: 20 min; BAKE: 30 min

6 SERVINGS

Make soft bread crumbs by tearing fresh slices of bread by hand or in a food processor. Gouda is a mild cheese from Holland with a nutlike flavor. Its creamy texture is due to a high milk fat content. Serve slices of dark pumpernickel or caraway rye bread with this smooth-textured pie.

2 small eggplants (about 1 pound each), peeled and cut into 3/4-inch pieces

1 cup shredded smoked Gouda cheese (4 ounces)

1/2 cup ricotta cheese

1/4 cup fine soft bread crumbs

1 tablespoon chopped fresh or 1 teaspoon dried basil leaves

1/2 teaspoon salt

1/8 teaspoon pepper

1 clove garlic, finely chopped

3 eggs, beaten

1. Heat oven to 350°. Grease pie plate, 9 × 1 1/4 inches.

2. Place steamer basket in 1/2 inch water in saucepan or skillet (water should not touch bottom of basket). Place eggplant in steamer basket. Cover tightly and heat to boiling; reduce heat. Steam 5 to 7 minutes or until tender.

3. Place eggplant in large bowl; mash with fork. Stir in 3/4 cup of the Gouda cheese and the remaining ingredients. Spoon mixture into pie plate. Sprinkle with remaining 1/4 cup Gouda cheese.

4. Bake uncovered about 30 minutes or until knife inserted in center comes out clean.

1 Serving: Calories 180 (Calories from Fat 90); Fat 10g (Saturated 6g); Cholesterol 130mg; Sodium 480mg; Carbohydrate 14g (Dietary Fiber 3g); Protein 12g.

Easy Spinach Pie

PREP: 20 min; BAKE: 30 min

4 SERVINGS

Enjoy the delicious flavor of spinach soufflé without the risk! This makes a good main dish for entertaining—serve it with your favorite cheese sauce. A salad of fresh orange and onion slices sprinkled with toasted almonds completes the meal.

2 tablespoons margarine or butter

1 package (10 ounces) washed fresh spinach, finely chopped

1 small red bell pepper, chopped (1/2 cup)

3/4 cup milk

2 tablespoons all-purpose flour

1/2 teaspoon salt

1/8 teaspoon ground nutmeg

3 eggs

2 tablespoons grated Parmesan cheese

1. Heat oven to 350°. Grease pie plate, 9 × 1 1/4 inches.

2. Melt margarine in 12-inch skillet over medium heat. Cook spinach and bell pepper in margarine about 5 minutes, stirring occasionally, until spinach is wilted and bell pepper is crisp-tender.

3. Beat remaining ingredients except cheese until smooth; pour into skillet. Stir mixture; pour into pie plate.

4. Bake uncovered about 30 minutes or until center is set. Sprinkle with cheese. Serve immediately.

1 Serving: Calories 165 (Calories from Fat 100); Fat 11g (Saturated 3g); Cholesterol 165mg; Sodium 530mg; Carbohydrate 9g (Dietary Fiber 2g); Protein 10g.

Vegetarian Substitutions

Here is a substitution list if you want to replace meat or an animal by-product with a vegetarian ingredient. Check the "Going Meatless: A Glossary" on page 244 for definitions of the vegetarian ingredients that might not be familiar to you.

For	Substitute
Meat, poultry, fish or seafood	Cheese, eggs, legumes, mushrooms, nut butters (almond, cashew, peanut, sesame), nuts, seeds, seitan, tempeh, texturized soy protein, tofu
Meat, poultry, fish or seafood broth	Miso, fruit juices, vegetable juices, vegetable broth, wine
Gelatin	Agar-agar, arrowroot, ground nuts, ground peanuts, ground seeds
Cheese	Soy cheeses
Eggs	Tofu
Milk	Soy milk, nut milk, rice milk

Twice-Baked Cheese Potatoes

Prep: 1 hr 25 min; Bake: 20 min

4 servings

The best baking potatoes are the white Russets or Idaho varieties recognized by their long shape. This type of potato bakes into dry, fluffy perfection. If you are in a hurry, microwave the potatoes on High 12 to 14 minutes and finish the filled potato shells in the oven.

4 medium baking potatoes

1/2 can (15- to 16-ounce size) great northern or cannellini beans, rinsed and drained

1/4 cup sour cream

1/4 cup chopped fresh chives

3 cups chopped spinach (4 ounces)

1 cup ricotta cheese

1/2 cup shredded Cheddar cheese (2 ounces)

3/4 cup chopped onions (1 1/2 medium)

2 teaspoons margarine or butter, softened

2 eggs

1 tablespoon bacon flavor bits or chips, if desired

1. Heat oven to 375°. Pierce potatoes with fork. Bake 1 to 1 1/4 hours until tender. Cool just until easy to handle. Cut potatoes lengthwise in half; scoop out inside, leaving a thin shell.

2. Mash potato and beans in medium bowl. Stir in 2 tablespoons of the sour cream, 2 tablespoons of the chives and remaining ingredients. Fill shells with potato mixture. Place in ungreased rectangular pan, 13 × 9 × 2 inches.

3. Bake uncovered 15 to 20 minutes or until hot and light brown. Top with remaining 2 tablespoons sour cream, chives and bacon bits.

1 Serving: Calories 420 (Calories from Fat 155); Fat 17g (Saturated 9g); Cholesterol 150mg; Sodium 380mg; Carbohydrate 51g (Dietary Fiber 7g); Protein 23g.

Twice-Baked Cheese Potatoes and Sweet and White Potatoes with Cilantro Cream (page 189)

Potato-Leek Gratin

PREP: 25 min; BAKE: 25 min

6 SERVINGS

Leeks look like overgrown green onions. The smaller the leek, the more tender it will be. Leeks have to be thoroughly washed before cooking due to the dirt that is trapped within their layers. After removing the root and leaf ends, cut the leek from top to bottom. Rinse under cold water, separating the leaves with your fingers.

2 1/2 cups milk

2 cloves garlic, finely chopped

1 teaspoon salt

1/4 teaspoon pepper

2 pounds potatoes, cut into 1/4-inch slices

3 medium leeks, sliced (2 cups)

1/4 cup sour cream

1 tablespoon Dijon mustard

1 cup shredded Swiss cheese (4 ounces)

1. Heat oven to 425°. Grease 2-quart gratin dish or shallow baking dish.

2. Heat milk, garlic, salt and pepper to simmering in 12-inch skillet over medium-low heat; add potatoes and leeks. Cook uncovered about 15 minutes, stirring frequently, just until tender.

3. Spoon potato mixture into gratin dish. Mix sour cream and mustard; spoon over potato mixture. Sprinkle with cheese. Bake uncovered 20 to 25 minutes or until bubbly around edge and golden brown on top.

1 Serving: Calories 235 (Calories from Fat 80); Fat 9g (Saturated 5g); Cholesterol 30mg; Sodium 530mg; Carbohydrate 29g (Dietary Fiber 2g); Protein 11g.

> POTATO-LEEK GRATIN WITH HAM: *Add 1 cup diced fully cooked smoked turkey ham with leeks in step 2. Continue as directed.*

Sweet and White Potatoes with Cilantro Cream

PREP: 15 min; BAKE: 50 min

6 SERVINGS

Handle hot chilies with care and be sure to wash your hands thoroughly after chopping. A jalapeño chili is a good choice for this recipe. If fresh chilies are not available, use a four-ounce can of green chilies, drained, for the fresh green chili.

4 medium baking potatoes (1 1/2 pounds)

4 medium sweet potatoes or yams (1 1/2 pounds)

2 tablespoons margarine or butter, melted

1 teaspoon salt

1 container (8 ounces) sour cream

2 tablespoons chopped fresh chives

1 tablespoon finely chopped cilantro

1 tablespoon lime juice

1 small green chili, seeded and finely chopped (1 tablespoon)

1. Heat oven to 400°. Grease rectangular baking dish, 11 × 7 × 1 1/2 inches.

2. Peel baking potatoes and sweet potatoes; cut into 1/4-inch slices. Spread potatoes in baking dish. Drizzle with margarine, and sprinkle with salt; stir to coat.

3. Cover and bake about 45 minutes or until potatoes are tender.

4. Mix remaining ingredients. Spoon sour cream mixture over potatoes. Bake uncovered 5 minutes.

1 Serving: Calories 235 (Calories from Fat 100); Fat 11g (Saturated 5g); Cholesterol 25mg; Sodium 460mg; Carbohydrate 34g (Dietary Fiber 3g); Protein 3g.

Mediterranean Oven Pancake

PREP: 10 min; BAKE: 25 min

4 SERVINGS

Greek olives, also known as Kalamata (or Calamata) olives, are richly flavored with a salty tang. They make a nice substitute for meat due to their meaty texture, which holds up well during cooking.

2 tablespoons margarine or butter

1/2 cup all-purpose flour

1/2 cup milk

1/4 teaspoon Italian seasoning

1/4 teaspoon salt

2 eggs

1 teaspoon margarine or butter

2 cups julienne strips zucchini

1 package (4 ounces) feta cheese, crumbled

10 Greek olives, pitted and cut in half

1. Heat oven to 425°. Heat 2 tablespoons margarine in pie plate, 9 × 1 1/4 inches, in oven about 4 minutes or until hot and bubbly.

2. Beat flour, milk, Italian seasoning, salt and eggs with hand beater until well blended. Pour into pie plate. Bake uncovered 20 to 25 minutes or until side of pancake is puffed and deep golden brown.

3. While pancake is baking, melt 1 teaspoon margarine in 10-inch skillet over medium heat. Cook zucchini in margarine about 2 minutes, stirring frequently, until crisp-tender. Carefully stir in cheese.

4. Spoon zucchini mixture onto center of pancake. Sprinkle with olives.

1 Serving: Calories 255 (Calories from Fat 155); Fat 17g (Saturated 7g); Cholesterol 135mg; Sodium 680mg; Carbohydrate 17g (Dietary Fiber 1g); Protein 10g.

Pasta: Selection, Storage and Cooking

SELECTION

Pasta is available in three forms: dried, fresh and frozen. Dried pasta is usually found prepackaged or in self-serve bulk form, while fresh pasta can be found in the refrigerated section of the supermarket. The most common varieties of frozen pasta are lasagna noodles, egg noodles and filled tortellini or ravioli.

- When purchasing dried pasta, look for smooth, unbroken pasta.

- Avoid dried pasta with a marblelike surface (many fine lines); this indicates a problem with how it dried and it may fall apart during cooking.

- When purchasing fresh pasta, look for smooth, unbroken pasta with consistent color throughout the shape. Although fresh pasta should appear dry, it shouldn't appear brittle or crumbly. Avoid packages containing moisture droplets or liquid, which could indicate molding or mushy pasta.

- When purchasing frozen pasta, avoid packages containing ice crystals or those in which the pasta pieces are frozen together in a solid mass. Avoid pasta that is freezer burned (dry, white spots).

STORAGE

Uncooked Dried Pasta

Most dried pasta can be stored indefinitely, but for optimum quality and flavor, we recommend a one- to two-year storage time.

- Store in original packaging or transfer to air-tight glass or plastic containers and label contents with starting storage date.

- Store in a cool (60°F or less), dry location.

Uncooked Fresh Pasta

Fresh pasta is perishable and should be stored in the refrigerator. Most fresh pasta packages carry use-by or expiration dates.

- Store unopened pasta in original packaging.

- Cover opened, unused portions of pasta tightly to avoid drying.

Uncooked Frozen Pasta

Frozen pasta should be stored in the freezer until ready to cook.

- Store unopened pasta in original packaging.

- Store opened, unused portions tightly sealed to avoid freezer burn and drying.

- Freeze unopened pasta for up to nine months.

- Freeze opened pasta for up to three months.

Cooked Dried, Fresh and Frozen Pasta

To prevent sticking, cooked pasta can be tossed with a small amount of oil. Store in tightly sealed containers or plastic bags in the refrigerator for up to five days.

COOKING

Always cook pasta uncovered at a fast and continuous boil, using plenty of water. This allows the pasta to move freely, promoting even cooking. Be sure the water is boiling before adding pasta.

- Do not add oil to the cooking water; sauces will not cling to oil-coated pasta.
- Salting the cooking water is optional and not necessary for the proper cooking of pasta.
- Use at least one quart water (four cups) for every four ounces of pasta.
- Follow package directions for cooking times. Fresh pasta cooks faster than dried pasta. Cooked pasta should be tender but firm to the bite (al dente).
- Stir pasta frequently to prevent sticking.
- Do not rinse pasta after draining unless stated in the recipe. Pasta is usually rinsed when it is to be used in salads.

Basic Pasta Yields

Uncooked	Cooked	Servings
Macaroni 6 or 7 ounces (2 cups)	4 cups	4 to 6
Spaghetti 7 to 8 ounces	4 cups	4 to 6
Noodles 8 ounces (4 to 5 cups)	4 to 5 cups	4 to 6

Pasta Substitutions

Type of Pasta	Substitution
Fettuccine	Linguine
Spaghetti	Vermicelli or angel hair
Rosamarina (orzo)	Acini de Pepe
Rotini	Rotelle or radiatore
Penne	Mostaccioli or ziti
Farfalle (bow-ties)	Rotini or rotelle
Wagon Wheel	Radiatore, rotini or rotelle

Pasta Cooking Chart

Dry Pasta Type	Cooking Time in Minutes	Dry Pasta Type	Cooking Time in Minutes
Acini de Pepe	5 to 6	Rosamarina (orzo)	8 to 10
Angel Hair	5 to 6	Rotelle	10 to 12
Egg Noodles (regular and wide)	8 to 10 regular (10 to 12 extra-wide)	Rotini	8 to 10
Elbow Macaroni	8 to 10	Small Shells	9 to 11
Farfalle (bow-ties)	13 to 15	Soba (buckwheat)	6 to 7
Fettuccine	11 to 13	Spaghetti	8 to 10
Fusilli	11 to 13	Vermicelli	5 to 7
Japanese Curly Noodles	4 to 5	Wagon Wheel	10 to 12
Jumbo Shells	12 to 15	Ziti	14 to 15
Lasagna Noodles	12 to 15		
Linguine	9 to 13		
Mafalde (mini-lasagna noodles)	8 to 10	**Fresh Pasta Type (Purchased)**	**Cooking Time in Minutes**
Manicotti	10 to 12	Angel Hair	1 to 2
Medium Shells	9 to 11	Farfalle (bow-ties)	2 to 3
Mostaccioli	12 to 14	Fettuccine	1 to 2
Penne	9 to 13	Lasagna	2 to 3
Radiatore	9 to 11	Linguine	1 to 2
Rigatoni	12 to 15	Ravioli	6 to 8
		Tortellini	8 to 10

Rice and Bean Bake

PREP: 8 min; BAKE: 1 hr 5 min

4 SERVINGS

One cup of cooked regular white rice supplies about 200 calories, is virtually fat-free and is an excellent source of complex carbohydrates. Combine rice with beans and you have a tasty dish that is also a good source of dietary fiber.

1 cup uncooked regular long grain rice

1 1/2 cups boiling water

1 tablespoon vegetable or chicken bouillon granules

1 1/2 teaspoons chopped fresh or 1/2 teaspoon dried marjoram leaves

1 medium onion, chopped (1/2 cup)

1 can (15 to 16 ounces) kidney beans, undrained

1 package (10 ounces) frozen lima beans, thawed and drained

1/2 cup shredded Cheddar cheese (2 ounces)

1. Heat oven to 350°.

2. Mix all ingredients except cheese in ungreased 2-quart casserole.

3. Cover and bake 1 hour to 1 hour 5 minutes or until liquid is absorbed; stir. Sprinkle with cheese.

1 Serving: Calories 380 (Calories from Fat 55); Fat 6g (Saturated 4g); Cholesterol 15mg; Sodium 1450mg; Carbohydrate 74g (Dietary Fiber 11g); Protein 19g.

Broccoli-Rice Bake

PREP: 10 min; BAKE: 30 min

6 SERVINGS

Cream of mushroom or asparagus soup are also good in this broccoli dish. To save time, use 1 1/2 pounds frozen cut-up broccoli pieces, thawed, for the fresh broccoli. Omit cooking the broccoli and just start with step 2.

1 1/2 pounds broccoli, cut into bite-size pieces

2 cups uncooked instant brown rice

1 can (14 1/2 ounces) ready-to-serve vegetable broth

1 can (10 3/4 ounces) condensed cream of broccoli soup

1 jar (2 ounces) diced pimientos, drained

1/4 teaspoon pepper

2 tablespoons firm margarine or butter

1/2 cup Bisquick® Original baking mix

1. Heat oven to 425°. Heat 1 inch water to boiling in 2-quart saucepan; add broccoli. Heat to boiling; reduce heat to medium. Cover and cook about 5 minutes or until crisp-tender; drain.

2. Mix broccoli, rice, broth, soup, pimientos and pepper in 2-quart casserole. Cover and bake 20 minutes.

3. Cut margarine into baking mix, using pastry blender or crisscrossing 2 knives, until crumbly. Sprinkle crumbly mixture over broccoli mixture. Bake uncovered 8 to 10 minutes or until top is light brown.

1 Serving: Calories 350 (Calories from Fat 90); Fat 10g (Saturated 3g); Cholesterol 2mg; Sodium 830mg; Carbohydrate 62g (Dietary Fiber 6g); Protein 9g.

> CHICKEN-BROCCOLI RICE BAKE: *Add 1 cup cubed cooked chicken or turkey with the broccoli in step 2. Continue as directed.*

Bulgur-Stuffed Peppers

PREP: 20 min; BAKE: 20 min

4 SERVINGS

Bulgur, also known as bulgur wheat, is a delicious wheat product consisting of wheat kernels that have been steamed, dried and crushed. It has a tender, chewy texture and is high in fiber, niacin and iron.

2 large bell peppers

2 teaspoons margarine or butter

4 medium stalks celery, chopped (2 cups)

2 medium green onions, sliced (1/4 cup)

1 cup uncooked bulgur

1 can (14 1/2 ounces) ready-to-serve vegetable broth

1/2 teaspoon lemon pepper seasoning salt

1 cup shredded Colby–Monterey Jack cheese (4 ounces)

1. Heat oven to 375°. Cut each bell pepper lengthwise in half; remove seeds and membranes. Heat 2 inches water to boiling in 2-quart saucepan. Add pepper halves. Cook uncovered 1 minute; drain.

2. Melt margarine in same saucepan over medium-high heat. Cook celery and 3 tablespoons of the onions in margarine about 5 minutes, stirring occasionally, until crisp-tender.

3. Stir in bulgur, 1 1/2 cups of the broth and the seasoning salt. Heat to boiling; reduce heat to low. Cover and simmer 6 to 7 minutes or until liquid is absorbed. Stir in 3/4 cup of the cheese.

4. Fill bell pepper halves with bulgur mixture. Place peppers, filled sides up, in ungreased square pan, 8 × 8 × 2 inches. Pour remaining broth into pan. Cover and bake 20 minutes. Sprinkle with remaining 1/4 cup cheese and 1 tablespoon onion.

1 Serving: Calories 250 (Calories from Fat 100); Fat 11g (Saturated 6g); Cholesterol 30mg; Sodium 700mg; Carbohydrate 34g (Dietary Fiber 8g); Protein 12g.

Triple Corn Squares with Bean Sauce

PREP: 10 min; BAKE: 30 min

6 SERVINGS

If you aren't in the mood for beans, top these corn squares with your favorite cheese sauce.

1 can (14 to 15 ounces) cream-style corn

1 can (8 ounces) whole kernel corn, drained

1 pouch (6 1/2 ounces) golden corn bread and muffin mix

1/3 cup margarine or butter, melted

2 eggs

1 can (15 ounces) black beans, rinsed and drained

1/3 cup salsa

Chopped cilantro, if desired

1. Heat oven to 400°. Grease rectangular baking dish, 11 × 7 × 1 1/2 inches.

2. Mix cream-style corn, whole kernel corn, muffin mix (dry), margarine and eggs. Pour into baking dish.

3. Bake uncovered about 30 minutes or until casserole springs back when touched lightly in center.

4. During last 5 minutes of baking, mix beans and salsa in 1-quart saucepan. Cook over medium heat, stirring occasionally, until hot. Cut casserole into squares; top with bean sauce. Sprinkle with cilantro; serve immediately.

1 Serving: Calories 380 (Calories from Fat 125); Fat 14g (Saturated 3g); Cholesterol 70mg; Sodium 830mg; Carbohydrate 58g (Dietary Fiber 6g); Protein 12g.

TRIPLE CORN SQUARES WITH CHICKEN SAUCE: *Omit the black beans. Increase salsa to 3/4 cup. Heat 1 1/2 cups diced cooked chicken or turkey with salsa in step 3. Continue as directed.*

Triple Corn Squares with Bean Sauce

Baked Layered Polenta

PREP: 20 min; BAKE: 30 min

6 SERVINGS

Polenta is made from ground cornmeal and has been a staple of Italian cuisine for generations. It can be layered and baked, sliced and panfried or served as a side dish with a little margarine or butter.

1 package (6.6 ounces) polenta

3 1/2 cups water

1 teaspoon salt

**1 1/2 teaspoons chopped fresh or
1/2 teaspoon dried oregano leaves**

1 tablespoon olive or vegetable oil

**2 medium zucchini, coarsely chopped
(3 cups)**

**1 container (12 ounces) refrigerated
marinara sauce**

1 cup shredded mozzarella cheese (4 ounces)

1. Heat oven to 375°. Grease rectangular baking dish, 11 × 7 × 1 1/2 inches.

2. Cook polenta in salted water as directed on package; stir in oregano. Spread in baking dish.

3. Heat oil in nonstick 12-inch skillet over medium-high heat. Cook zucchini in oil 5 to 7 minutes, stirring occasionally, until crisp-tender. Stir in marinara sauce; reduce heat to medium. Cook about 5 minutes, stirring occasionally, until thickened.

4. Spoon zucchini mixture over polenta. Sprinkle with cheese. Bake uncovered about 30 minutes or until bubbly around edges.

1 Serving: Calories 245 (Calories from Fat 70); Fat 8g (Saturated 3g); Cholesterol 10mg; Sodium 1380mg; Carbohydrate 38g (Dietary Fiber 4g); Protein 9g.

> BAKED LAYERED POLENTA WITH CHICKEN: *Cook 2 skinless, boneless chicken breast halves, cut into 3/4-inch pieces, in oil in step 3 until no longer pink. Add zucchini and continue as directed.*

Cheese Grits

PREP: 20 min; BAKE: 40 min;
STAND: 10 min

6 SERVINGS

American as apple pie, grits are solidly entrenched in Southern cuisine. Grits are the product of coarsely ground corn and are generally eaten as a cereal or side dish. Here, they take center stage.

2 cups milk

2 cups water

1/2 teaspoon salt

1/4 teaspoon pepper

1 cup uncooked white hominy quick grits

1 1/2 cups shredded Cheddar cheese (6 ounces)

2 medium green onions, sliced (1/4 cup)

2 large eggs, slightly beaten

1 tablespoon margarine or butter

1/4 teaspoon paprika

1. Heat oven to 350°. Grease 1 1/2-quart casserole.

2. Heat milk, water, salt and pepper to boiling in 2-quart saucepan. Gradually add grits, stirring constantly; reduce heat. Simmer uncovered about 5 minutes, stirring frequently, until thickened. Stir in cheese and onions.

3. Stir 1 cup of the hot mixture into eggs; stir back into remaining hot mixture in saucepan. Pour into casserole. Dot with margarine. Sprinkle with paprika.

4. Bake uncovered 35 to 40 minutes or until set. Let stand 10 minutes.

1 Serving: Calories 295 (Calories from Fat 135); Fat 15g (Saturated 8g); Cholesterol 105mg; Sodium 830mg; Carbohydrate 26g (Dietary Fiber 0g); Protein 14g.

Top 5 Reasons to be a Vegetarian

1. Reduces risk for some diseases, such as obesity, high blood pressure and heart disease

2. Includes the benefits of a low-fat, high-fiber diet

3. Eat more fruits, vegetables and grains

4. All the nutrition, without the meat!

5. Live a more healthful lifestyle

Spaghetti Basil Torte

PREP: 15 min; BAKE: 30 min; STAND: 15 min

8 SERVINGS

This impressive looking torte is deceptively easy to make and a perfect dish to serve when you're entertaining. If you like ripe olives, add a can (four ounces) of sliced ripe olives to the spaghetti mixture. Serve with whole green beans and warm crusty bread.

1 package (16 ounces) spaghetti

1/2 cup grated Parmesan cheese

1/2 cup ricotta cheese

1 tablespoon Italian seasoning

2 eggs, beaten

1/4 cup chopped fresh or 1 1/2 teaspoons dried basil leaves

2 medium tomatoes, each cut into 5 slices

4 slices (1 ounce each) provolone cheese, cut in half

1. Heat oven to 350°. Spray springform pan, 9 × 3 inches, with cooking spray. Cook and drain spaghetti as directed on package. Rinse with cold water; drain.

2. Toss spaghetti, Parmesan cheese, ricotta cheese, Italian seasoning and eggs until spaghetti is well coated.

3. Press half of the spaghetti mixture in bottom of pan. Sprinkle with half of the basil. Layer with half of the tomato and cheese slices. Press remaining spaghetti mixture on top. Sprinkle with remaining basil. Layer with remaining tomato and cheese slices.

4. Bake uncovered 30 minutes until hot and light brown. Let stand 15 minutes. Remove side of pan. Cut torte into wedges.

1 Serving: Calories 335 (Calories from Fat 80); Fat 9g (Saturated 5g); Cholesterol 75mg; Sodium 270mg; Carbohydrate 48g (Dietary Fiber 2g); Protein 17g.

Alfredo Pasta Pie with Toasted French Bread Crust

PREP: 15 min; BAKE: 20 min; STAND: 5 min

6 SERVINGS

What a delicious way to use up leftover French bread! It becomes a toasted crust for this creamy pasta pie. Just add a vegetable or salad and your meal is complete.

4 ounces uncooked capellini (angel hair) pasta

18 slices French bread, about 1/4 inch thick

2 tablespoons margarine or butter, softened

3/4 cup shredded Swiss cheese (3 ounces)

2 tablespoons chopped fresh or 2 teaspoons dried basil leaves

1 container (10 ounces) refrigerated Alfredo sauce

3 medium roma (plum) tomatoes, chopped (1 cup)

2 medium green onions, sliced (1/4 cup)

1 tablespoon grated Romano or Parmesan cheese

1. Heat oven to 400°. Cook and drain pasta as directed on package.

2. While pasta is cooking, brush bread with margarine. Line bottom and side of pie plate, 10 × 1 1/2 inches, with bread, margarine sides up and slightly overlapping slices. Bake about 10 minutes or until light brown.

3. Reduce oven temperature to 350°. Stir Swiss cheese and 1 tablespoon of the basil into Alfredo sauce. Toss sauce and pasta. Spoon into baked crust.

4. Mix tomatoes, onions and remaining 1 tablespoon basil. Sprinkle over pasta mixture; lightly press onto surface. Sprinkle with Romano cheese.

5. Bake 15 to 20 minutes or until hot. Let stand 5 minutes before cutting.

1 Serving: Calories 365 (Calories from Fat 215); Fat 24g (Saturated 13g); Cholesterol 60mg; Sodium 370mg; Carbohydrate 26g (Dietary Fiber 1g); Protein 12g.

Vegetable Tetrazzini

PREP: 15 min; BAKE: 40 min

6 SERVINGS

If you're watching your fat intake, substitute 2 cups fat-free half-and-half for the half-and-half, reduce the margarine from 1/4 cup to 2 tablespoons and use 1 cup reduced-fat versus regular Cheddar cheese.

1 package (7 ounces) spaghetti

2 cups vegetable or chicken broth

2 cups half-and-half

1/2 cup all-purpose flour

1/4 cup margarine or butter

1/2 teaspoon salt

1/4 teaspoon pepper

2 cups frozen mixed vegetables

1 can (2 1/4 ounces) sliced ripe olives

1/2 cup slivered almonds

1/2 cup shredded Cheddar cheese (2 ounces)

1. Heat oven to 350°. Cook and drain spaghetti as directed on package. Rinse with cold water; drain.

2. Mix broth, half-and-half, flour, margarine, salt and pepper in 3-quart saucepan. Heat to boiling over medium heat, stirring constantly. Boil and stir 1 minute. Stir in spaghetti, vegetables and olives. Spread in ungreased 2-quart casserole. Sprinkle with almonds and cheese.

3. Bake uncovered 25 to 30 minutes or until hot and bubbly.

1 Serving: Calories 435 (Calories from Fat 205); Fat 23g (Saturated 10g); Cholesterol 40mg; Sodium 750mg; Carbohydrate 49g (Dietary Fiber 6g); Protein 14g.

CHICKEN TETRAZZINI: *Omit the frozen mixed vegetables. Add 2 cups diced cooked chicken or turkey with the spaghetti in step 2. Continue as directed.*

Layered Spinach Fettuccine with Tomato Cream Sauce

PREP: 10 min; BAKE 20 min

6 SERVINGS

Keep a few packages of refrigerated pasta and containers of sauce on hand for quick and delicious meals. For an Italian party, use a green bell pepper and regular fettuccine for a "red, white and green" dish.

1 package (9 ounces) refrigerated spinach fettuccine

2 cups sliced mushrooms (6 ounces)

1 large yellow bell pepper, chopped (1 1/2 cups)

1 small onion, finely chopped (1/4 cup)

2 containers (10 ounces each) refrigerated plum tomato cream sauce

4 ounces sliced mozzarella cheese

4 medium roma (plum) tomatoes, sliced

1. Heat oven to 375°. Grease 2-quart casserole.

2. Cook and drain fettuccine as directed on package. Spread fettuccine in casserole. Top with mushrooms, bell pepper and onion. Pour sauce over vegetables. Top with cheese and tomatoes.

3. Bake uncovered about 20 minutes or until bubbly around edge.

1 Serving: Calories 300 (Calories from Fat 90); Fat 10g (Saturated 5g); Cholesterol 65mg; Sodium 620mg; Carbohydrate 41g (Dietary Fiber 3g); Protein 15g.

LAYERED CHICKEN-SPINACH FETTUCCINE WITH TOMATO CREAM SAUCE: *Sprinkle 2 cups cubed cooked chicken or turkey over fettuccine step 2. Continue as directed.*

Sunny-Side-Up Stroganoff

PREP: 15 min; BAKE: 20 min

4 SERVINGS

Change the flavor of this brunch casserole by using a different flavor of noodles and sauce mix. To keep the eggs "sunny-side-up," break the egg into a sauce dish or saucer. Carefully slip the egg into the indentation.

2 packages (4 ounces each) stroganoff noodles and sauce mix

1 teaspoon Worcestershire sauce

4 eggs

1/4 teaspoon salt

1/4 teaspoon pepper

1 medium tomato, chopped (3/4 cup)

2 tablespoons chopped fresh parsley

1. Heat oven to 400°. Grease square pan, 8 × 8 × 2 inches.

2. Prepare noodles and sauce mix as directed on package; stir in Worcestershire sauce. Spread mixture in pan. Make 4 indentations in noodle mixture, using back of spoon. Break 1 egg into each indentation. Sprinkle with salt and pepper.

3. Bake uncovered 15 to 20 minutes or until egg whites and yolks are firm, not runny. Sprinkle with tomato and parsley.

1 Serving: Calories 370 (Calories from Fat 145); Fat 16g (Saturated 6g); Cholesterol 280mg; Sodium 1170mg; Carbohydrate 42g (Dietary Fiber 2g); Protein 17g.

Mom's Macaroni and Cheese

PREP: 10 min; BAKE: 30 min

5 SERVINGS

Process sharp American cheese loaf melts much better than natural Cheddar cheese and doesn't curdle or congeal when cooked, so this classic favorite stays rich, smooth and creamy.

**1 1/2 cups uncooked elbow macaroni
(5 ounces)**

2 tablespoons margarine or butter

1 small onion, chopped (1/4 cup)

1/2 teaspoon salt

1/4 teaspoon pepper

1/4 cup all-purpose flour

1 3/4 cups milk

**6 ounces process sharp American cheese
loaf, cut into 1/2-inch cubes**

1. Heat oven to 375°. Cook and drain macaroni as directed on package.

2. While macaroni is cooking, melt margarine in 2-quart saucepan over medium heat. Cook onion, salt and pepper in margarine, stirring occasionally, until onion is crisp-tender. Mix flour and milk until smooth; stir into onion mixture. Heat to boiling, stirring constantly. Boil and stir 1 minute; remove from heat. Stir in cheese until melted. Stir in macaroni.

3. Spoon macaroni mixture into ungreased 1 1/2-quart casserole. Bake uncovered about 30 minutes or until bubbly and light brown.

1 Serving: Calories 380 (Calories from Fat 160); Fat 18g (Saturated 9g); Cholesterol 40mg; Sodium 820mg; Carbohydrate 41g (Dietary Fiber 2g); Protein 16g.

*Mom's Macaroni and Cheese
and Pizza Casserole (page 210)*

Pizza Casserole

PREP: 15 min; BAKE: 35 min

6 SERVINGS

This casserole will soon be a family favorite. Not only is it easy but the kids will love the wagon wheel pasta shape. If the kids don't care for ripe olives, just leave them out. Mafalda, which look like mini-lasagna noodles, can be used instead of the wagon wheels.

4 cups uncooked wagon wheel pasta (8 ounces)

1 jar (28 ounces) spaghetti sauce

1 can (8 ounces) mushroom stems and pieces, drained

1 can (2 1/4 ounces) sliced ripe olives, drained

1 cup shredded mozzarella cheese (4 ounces)

1. Heat oven to 350°. Cook and drain pasta as directed on package.

2. Mix pasta and remaining ingredients except cheese in ungreased 2 1/2-quart casserole.

3. Cover and bake about 30 minutes or until hot and bubbly. Sprinkle with cheese. Bake uncovered about 5 minutes or until cheese is melted.

1 Serving: Calories 350 (Calories from Fat 90); Fat 10g (Saturated 4g); Cholesterol 10mg; Sodium 980mg; Carbohydrate 57g (Dietary Fiber 4g); Protein 12g.

PIZZA TURKEY CASSEROLE: *Add 1 pound cooked ground turkey with remaining ingredients in step 2. Continue as directed.*

Two-Cheese Pasta Casserole

PREP: 15 min; BAKE: 40 min

8 SERVINGS

Ricotta cheese is smoother and just a tad sweeter than cottage cheese, but the two are almost always interchangeable if you use a small curd cottage cheese. Ricotta cheese is a good source of calcium and protein.

1 package (16 ounces) mostaccioli pasta

1 jar (26 to 30 ounces) spaghetti sauce

1 container (15 ounces) ricotta cheese

1 package (10 ounces) frozen chopped spinach, thawed and squeezed to drain

4 medium green onions, chopped (1/4 cup)

1/4 cup sliced pimiento-stuffed olives

2 tablespoons grated Parmesan cheese

1 tablespoon chopped fresh parsley or 1 teaspoon parsley flakes

1/8 teaspoon pepper

1. Heat oven to 375°. Cook and drain pasta as directed on package.

2. Mix pasta and remaining ingredients. Spoon into ungreased rectangular baking dish, 13 × 9 × 2 inches.

3. Cover and bake about 40 minutes or until hot and bubbly.

1 Serving: Calories 400 (Calories from Fat 90); Fat 10g (Saturated 4g); Cholesterol 15mg; Sodium 670mg; Carbohydrate 66g (Dietary Fiber 4g); Protein 16g.

Vegetable Manicotti

PREP: 20 min; BAKE: 1 hr

4 SERVINGS

To make this manicotti ahead of time, follow directions through step 3 and then cover and refrigerate up to 24 hours. You may need to add 10 to 15 minutes to the baking time if placing in the oven directly from the refrigerator.

12 uncooked manicotti shells

1 container (15 ounces) ricotta cheese

1 small zucchini, coarsely shredded (1 cup)

1 cup coarsely shredded carrots (1 1/2 medium)

1/2 cup shredded mozzarella cheese (2 ounces)

2 tablespoons chopped fresh parsley

2 teaspoons sugar

1 egg white, slightly beaten

1 jar (26 to 30 ounces) spaghetti sauce

2 tablespoons grated Parmesan cheese

1. Heat oven to 350°. Spray rectangular baking dish, 13 × 9 × 2 inches, with cooking spray. Cook and drain shells as directed on package.

2. While shells are cooking, mix remaining ingredients except spaghetti sauce and Parmesan cheese.

3. Fill each cooked shell with about 2 tablespoons vegetable mixture; place filled sides up in baking dish. Spoon spaghetti sauce over shells. Sprinkle with Parmesan cheese.

4. Cover and bake 50 to 60 minutes or until hot.

1 Serving: Calories 590 (Calories from Fat 170); Fat 19g (Saturated 9g); Cholesterol 40mg; Sodium 1180mg; Carbohydrate 84g (Dietary Fiber 6g); Protein 27g.

Lasagna Primavera

PREP: 20 min; BAKE: 1 HR; STAND: 15 min

8 SERVINGS

12 uncooked lasagna noodles

2 containers (10 ounces each) refrigerated Alfredo sauce

3 cups frozen broccoli flowerets, thawed and well drained

3 large carrots, coarsely shredded (2 cups)

1 can (14 1/2 ounces) diced tomatoes, well drained

2 medium bell peppers, cut into 1/2-inch pieces

1 container (15 ounces) ricotta cheese

1/2 cup grated Parmesan cheese

1 egg

1 package (16 ounces) shredded mozzarella cheese (4 cups)

1. Cook and drain noodles as directed on package.

2. Cut broccoli flowerets into bite-size pieces if necessary. Mix broccoli, carrots, tomatoes and bell peppers in large bowl. Mix ricotta cheese, Parmesan cheese and egg in small bowl.

3. Heat oven to 375°. Spoon 2/3 cup sauce in ungreased rectangular pan, 13 × 9 × 2 inches. Place 4 noodles over sauce. Spread half of cheese mixture, 2 1/2 cups of the vegetable mixture and randomly spoon 2/3 cup sauce in dollops over noodles. Sprinkle with 1 cup of the mozzarella cheese. Top with 4 noodles; spread with remaining cheese mixture, 2 1/2 cups of the vegetable mixture and randomly spoon 2/3 cup sauce in dollops over vegetables. Sprinkle with 1 cup mozzarella cheese. Top with remaining 4 noodles and vegetable mixture. Randomly spoon remaining sauce in dollops over the top. Sprinkle with remaining 2 cups mozzarella cheese.

4. Bake uncovered 45 minutes to 1 hour or until bubbly and hot in center. Let stand 15 minutes before cutting.

1 Serving: Calories 475 (Calories from Fat 180); Fat 20g (Saturated 10g); Cholesterol 75mg; Sodium 830mg; Carbohydrate 46g (Dietary Fiber 4g); Protein 32g.

Stacked Enchilada Bake

PREP: 10 min; BAKE: 20 min

6 SERVINGS

Kitchen scissors are a quick way to cut the tortillas into bite-size pieces. Shredded lettuce, chopped tomatoes, sour cream and chopped green onions make tasty "fixins" to top each serving.

12 corn tortillas (5 or 6 inches in diameter), torn into bite-size pieces

2 cans (15 to 16 ounces each) chili beans in sauce, undrained

1 can (10 ounces) enchilada sauce

1 1/2 cups shredded Monterey Jack cheese (6 ounces)

3 medium green onions, sliced (1/4 cup)

1. Heat oven to 400°. Grease 2-quart casserole.

2. Place half of the tortilla pieces in casserole; top with 1 can beans. Repeat layers. Pour enchilada sauce oven beans and tortilla pieces. Sprinkle with cheese and onions. Bake uncovered about 20 minutes or until bubbly around edge.

1 Serving: Calories 300 (Calories from Fat 90); Fat 10g (Saturated 6g); Cholesterol 25mg; Sodium 910mg; Carbohydrate 45g (Dietary Fiber 8g); Protein 16g.

Stacked Enchilada Bake

Bean Enchiladas

PREP: 15 min; BAKE: 25 min

6 SERVINGS

Flour tortillas come in several varieties from regular, to fat-free, to whole wheat and to a myriad of flavors such as pumpkin, spinach, cilantro and tomato. Not only do the flavored tortillas add a flavor twist but some, such as spinach and tomato, also add color.

1 can (16 ounces) whole tomatoes, undrained

1 medium onion, chopped (1/2 cup)

1 clove garlic, finely chopped

1/4 cup chopped fresh cilantro

1/8 teaspoon crushed red pepper

1 can (15 to 16 ounces) pinto beans, rinsed and drained

1 cup ricotta cheese

1 small green bell pepper, chopped (1/2 cup)

1 teaspoon ground cumin

6 flour tortillas (8 to 10 inches in diameter)

1/4 cup shredded Cheddar cheese (1 ounce)

1/4 cup shredded Monterey Jack cheese (1 ounce)

1. Heat oven to 375°. Grease rectangular baking dish, 11 × 7 × 1 1/2 inches.

2. Place tomatoes, onion and garlic in blender or food processor. Cover and blend on high speed until smooth. Mix blended tomato sauce, 2 tablespoons of the cilantro and the red pepper. Spread 1/2 cup tomato sauce in baking dish.

3. Mix beans, ricotta cheese, bell pepper, cumin and remaining 2 tablespoons cilantro. Spoon 1/2 cup bean mixture onto one side of each tortilla. Roll up tortillas; place seam sides down on tomato sauce in baking dish.

4. Spoon remaining tomato sauce over tortillas. Sprinkle with Cheddar and Monterey Jack cheeses. Bake 20 to 25 minutes or until tomato sauce is bubbly and cheese is melted.

1 Serving: Calories 290 (Calories from Fat 65); Fat 7g (Saturated 3g); Cholesterol 10mg; Sodium 570mg; Carbohydrate 48g (Dietary Fiber 8g); Protein 17g.

Lentil and Brown Rice Casserole

PREP: 10 min; BAKE: 1 hr 30 min

6 SERVINGS

The green beans are added frozen halfway through the cooking time to help maintain their bright green color and texture. This casserole is so easy, it's sure to become one of your dinner favorites.

3/4 cup dried lentils (6 ounces), sorted and rinsed

1/2 cup uncooked brown rice

2 1/2 cups vegetable or chicken broth

1 package (16 ounces) frozen cut green beans or broccoli cuts

1 cup shredded Cheddar cheese (4 ounces)

1. Heat oven to 375°. Mix lentils, rice and broth in 2-quart casserole. Cover and bake 1 hour.

2. Stir in frozen green beans. Cover and bake about 30 minutes or until liquid is absorbed and rice is tender. Sprinkle with cheese.

1 Serving: Calories 225 (Calories from Fat 65); Fat 7g (Saturated 5g); Cholesterol 20mg; Sodium 800mg; Carbohydrate 35g (Dietary Fiber 9g); Protein 14g.

6

Simple Side Dishes and Breads

Cheddar-Cornmeal Scones (page 232) and
Artichoke-Rosemary Bruschetta (page 237)

Herbed Broccoli

PREP: 10 min; COOK: 10 min

4 SERVINGS

Hooray for broccoli! This fresh green vegetable gets high marks for being an excellent source of vitamins A and C, calcium, iron and riboflavin.

1 pound broccoli, cut into 1-inch pieces*

2 tablespoons olive or vegetable oil

1 teaspoon chopped fresh or 1/4 teaspoon dried basil leaves

1 teaspoon chopped fresh or 1/4 teaspoon dried oregano leaves

1/2 teaspoon salt

1 clove garlic, finely chopped

2 medium roma (plum) tomatoes, chopped (2/3 cup)

1. Heat 1 inch water (salted if desired) to boiling in 3-quart saucepan. Add broccoli. Cover and heat to boiling; reduce heat. Simmer about 10 minutes or until crisp-tender; drain.

2. Heat oil in 10-inch skillet over medium heat. Add basil, oregano, salt, garlic and tomatoes; cook about 1 minute, stirring frequently, until hot. Pour over broccoli; toss.

*2 packages (10 ounces each) frozen chopped broccoli, cooked and drained, can be substituted for the fresh broccoli.

1 Serving: Calories 85 (Calories from Fat 65); Fat 7g (Saturated 1g); Cholesterol 0mg; Sodium 310mg; Carbohydrate 5g (Dietary Fiber 2g); Protein 2g.

Creamy Confetti Succotash

PREP: 10 min; COOK: 10 min

5 SERVINGS

Lima beans hail from Lima, Peru, where they were found by Europeans around the year 1500. Along with corn, limas are an essential ingredient in succotash. They are a good source of protein, phosphorus, potassium and iron.

1 tablespoon margarine or butter

1 small red or green bell pepper, chopped (1/2 cup)

2 medium green onions, sliced (1/4 cup)

2 cups fresh or frozen whole kernel corn

1 cup frozen baby lima beans

1/4 cup half-and-half

2 teaspoons fresh or 1/2 teaspoon dried marjoram leaves

1/4 teaspoon salt

1/8 teaspoon pepper

1. Melt margarine in 8-inch skillet over medium-high heat. Cook bell pepper and onions in margarine 2 to 3 minutes, stirring occasionally, until crisp-tender.

2. Stir in remaining ingredients; reduce heat to medium-low. Cover and cook 5 to 6 minutes, stirring occasionally, until vegetables are tender.

1 Serving: Calories 120 (Calories from Fat 35); Fat 4g (Saturated 1g); Cholesterol 5mg; Sodium 170mg; Carbohydrate 21g (Dietary Fiber 4g); Protein 4g.

Creamy Confetti Succotash

Roasted Baby Carrots

PREP: 5 min; BAKE: 40 min

6 SERVINGS

Roasting carrots makes them even sweeter because while they cook, more of the carrot starches turn into sugar. Another plus—carrots are very high in vitamin A.

4 teaspoons vegetable oil

1 tablespoon chopped fresh or 1 teaspoon dried thyme leaves

1/4 teaspoon garlic salt

1/8 teaspoon pepper

1 package (16 ounces) baby-cut carrots (6 cups)

1 package (8 ounces) baby-cut carrots (3 cups)

1. Heat oven to 425°. Spray rectangular pan, 13 × 9 × 2 inches, with cooking spray.

2. Mix all ingredients except carrots in large bowl; toss to coat. Spread carrots in pan.

3. Bake uncovered 35 to 40 minutes, stirring occasionally, until carrots are tender.

1 Serving: Calories 70 (Calories from Fat 30); Fat 3g (Saturated 0g); Cholesterol 0mg; Sodium 80mg; Carbohydrate 12g (Dietary Fiber 3g); Protein 1g.

Hot and Spicy Greens

PREP: 10 min; COOK: 10 min

6 SERVINGS

Collard greens are a form of cabbage, but instead of forming a head, they stay in a loose, leaf form. Collards are an excellent source of vitamins A and C as well as calcium and iron.

2 tablespoons margarine or butter

2 pounds collard greens or spinach, coarsely chopped

1 serrano chile, seeded and finely chopped

2 tablespoons finely chopped onion

1 to 2 teaspoons grated gingerroot

1. Melt margarine in Dutch oven over medium heat.

2. Cook remaining ingredients in margarine, stirring frequently, until greens and onion are tender; drain.

1 Serving: Calories 70 (Calories from Fat 35); Fat 4g (Saturated 1g); Cholesterol 0mg; Sodium 65mg; Carbohydrate 9g (Dietary Fiber 2g); Protein 2g.

Beyond Water: Flavor-Packed Rice and Grains

Using water for cooking rice and grains is only one of many possibilities. Other liquids can add interesting flavor to your finished dish. Some high-acid liquids, such as tomato juice and wine, should be combined with water because the amount of acid might increase the cook time. Be sure the flavored liquid you use to cook rice or grains goes well with the dish to which it is added or with which it is served. Try one of the following "liquid assets" in place of water in your recipe:

- **Fruit Juice:** Replace half or all of the amount of water with apple or orange juice or fruit juice blends such as pineapple-orange or apple-cranberry. This makes an easy side dish or a flavorful addition to a salad or dessert.

- **Vegetable Juice:** Replace half of the amount of water with tomato, spicy eight-vegetable, carrot or other vegetable juice. This is good as a side dish or in casseroles, soups and salads.

- **Wine:** Replace half of the amount of water with white or red wine. A sweeter white wine is good for salads and dessert dishes; a hearty red wine is great in casseroles and soups.

- **Broth:** A good-quality canned or home-made vegetable broth can be used for cooking any rice or grain. It can replace all of the water in your recipe.

- **Milk:** Replace half or all of the amount of water with milk when cooking rice and grains. This can make a rich, hearty hot cereal or a base for a side dish or dessert. Unsweetened canned coconut milk also can be used. For a richer flavor, use all coconut milk. Rice and grains cooked in coconut milk can be used as a side dish or dessert.

Roasted Rosemary-Onion Potatoes

PREP: 12 min; BAKE: 25 min

4 SERVINGS

Potato lovers may opt to eat this aromatic, savory combination with a salad and call it dinner! However, if you'd like a bit more, serve the potatoes with grilled chicken breasts.

2 tablespoons chopped fresh or 2 teaspoons dried rosemary leaves

2 tablespoons olive or vegetable oil

1 teaspoon chopped fresh or 1/4 teaspoon dried thyme leaves

1/4 teaspoon salt

1/8 teaspoon pepper

1 small onion, finely chopped (1/4 cup)

4 medium potatoes (1 1/3 pounds), cut into 1-inch pieces

1. Heat oven to 450°. Grease jelly roll pan, 15 1/2 × 10 1/2 × 1 inch.

2. Mix all ingredients except potatoes in large bowl. Add potatoes; toss to coat. Spread potatoes in single layer in pan.

3. Bake uncovered 20 to 25 minutes, turning occasionally, until potatoes are light brown and tender when pierced with fork.

1 Serving: Calories 195 (Calories from Fat 65); Fat 7g (Saturated 1g); Cholesterol 0mg; Sodium 155mg; Carbohydrate 33g (Dietary Fiber 3g); Protein 3g.

Swiss Potato Patties

PREP: 45 min; COOK: 16 min

8 PATTIES

Pair these potato patties with Herbed Broccoli (page 220) and fresh tomato slices for a great meatless meal.

4 medium potatoes (1 1/3 pounds)

1 cup shredded Swiss cheese (4 ounces)

1/4 teaspoon salt

1/4 teaspoon pepper

1 tablespoon margarine or butter

1. Heat 1 inch water (salted if desired) to boiling in 3-quart saucepan. Add potatoes. Cover and heat to boiling; reduce heat. Simmer 30 to 35 minutes or until tender; drain.

2. Peel and shred potatoes. Mix potatoes, cheese, salt and pepper.

3. Melt margarine in 10-inch skillet over medium-high heat. Scoop one half of potato mixture by 1/3 cupfuls into skillet; flatten to 1/2-inch thickness. Cook about 8 minutes, turning once, until golden brown. Repeat with remaining potato mixture.

1 Patty: Calories 125 (Calories from Fat 45); Fat 5g (Saturated 3g); Cholesterol 15mg; Sodium 130mg; Carbohydrate 16g (Dietary Fiber 1g); Protein 5g.

Roasted Rosemary-Onion Potatoes with Swiss Potato Patties

Sweet Potato Wedges

PREP: 10 min; BAKE: 30 min

4 SERVINGS

These oven-fried sweet potato wedges are loaded with vitamin A and good amounts of potassium and calcium. August to October is the best time to buy sweet potatoes because they are at their peak and are the most moist.

4 medium sweet potatoes (1 1/2 pounds), cut lengthwise into 1/2-inch wedges

2 tablespoons vegetable oil

1/2 teaspoon salt

1/4 teaspoon pepper

1. Heat oven to 450°. Grease jelly roll pan, 15 1/2 × 10 1/2 × 1 inch.

2. Toss potatoes and oil in large bowl. Sprinkle with salt and pepper. Spread potatoes in single layer in pan.

3. Bake uncovered 25 to 30 minutes, turning occasionally, until potatoes are golden brown and tender when pierced with fork.

1 Serving: Calories 155 (Calories from Fat 65); Fat 7g (Saturated 1g); Cholesterol 0mg; Sodium 300mg; Carbohydrate 25g (Dietary Fiber 3g); Protein 1g.

Fettuccine and Broccoli with Sharp Cheddar Sauce

PREP: 5 min; COOK: 15 min

6 SERVINGS

This recipe leads a double life! Not only is this a tasty side dish for six, but it makes a splendid main dish for four. If you don't have roasted red bell peppers, use canned pimientos.

6 ounces uncooked fettuccine, broken into thirds

2 cups frozen broccoli cuts

1 jar (5 ounces) process sharp cheese spread

1/4 cup milk

2 tablespoons 1/4-inch strips drained roasted red bell peppers (from 7-ounce jar)

1. Cook and drain fettuccine as directed on package, except add broccoli about 2 minutes before fettuccine is done; set aside.

2. Mix cheese spread and milk in saucepan. Cook over medium heat 1 to 3 minutes, stirring frequently, until smooth. Stir in fettuccine, broccoli and bell peppers until coated.

1 Serving: Calories 200 (Calories from Fat 80); Fat 9g (Saturated 5g); Cholesterol 50mg; Sodium 380mg; Carbohydrate 21g (Dietary Fiber 1g); Protein 10g.

Fettuccine and Broccoli with Sharp Cheddar Sauce

Hearty Multigrain Biscuits

PREP: 10 min; BAKE: 12 min

10 BISCUITS

Whole wheat flour still contains the wheat germ and is therefore light brown in color and has a full-flavored, slightly nutty taste. Store whole wheat flour in the refrigerator or freezer to prevent it from becoming rancid.

3/4 cup whole wheat flour

1/2 cup all-purpose flour

1/2 cup cornmeal

3 teaspoons baking powder

1/2 teaspoon salt

1/4 cup shortening

1/2 cup quick-cooking or old-fashioned oats

About 3/4 cup skim milk

1. Heat oven to 450°. Mix flours, cornmeal, baking powder and salt in large bowl. Cut in shortening, using pastry blender or crisscrossing 2 knives, until mixture looks like fine crumbs. Stir in oats. Stir in just enough milk so dough leaves side of bowl and forms a ball.

2. Turn dough onto lightly floured surface. Knead lightly 10 times. Roll or pat 1/2 inch thick. Cut with floured 2 1/2-inch round cutter. Place on ungreased cookie sheet about 1 inch apart for crusty sides, touching for soft sides. Brush with milk and sprinkle with oats if desired.

3. Bake 10 to 12 minutes or until golden brown. Immediately remove from cookie sheet. Serve warm.

1 Biscuit: Calories 145 (Calories from Fat 55); Fat 6g (Saturated 1g); Cholesterol 0mg; Sodium 270mg; Carbohydrate 21g (Dietary Fiber 2g); Protein 4g.

Banana-Gingerbread Muffins

PREP: 5 min; BAKE: 20 min

16 MUFFINS

The riper the bananas, the more banana flavor these gingery muffins will have. For a quick snack or dessert, frost muffins with canned vanilla frosting.

1 package (14 1/2 ounces) gingerbread cake and cookie mix

2 ripe medium bananas, mashed (1 cup)

3/4 cup quick-cooking oats

3/4 cup water

2 eggs

1. Heat oven to 375°. Grease bottoms only of 16 medium muffin cups, 2 1/2 × 1 1/4 inches, or line with paper baking cups.

2. Mix all ingredients until well blended. Divide batter evenly among muffin cups.

3. Bake 15 to 20 minutes or until toothpick inserted in center comes out clean. Immediately remove from pan.

1 Muffin: Calories 145 (Calories from Fat 35); Fat 4g (Saturated 1g); Cholesterol 25mg; Sodium 190mg; Carbohydrate 25g (Dietary Fiber 0g); Protein 2g.

Double Corn Muffins

PREP: 10 min; BAKE: 20 min

8 MUFFINS

The most commonly available cornmeal is either white or yellow cornmeal, but some specialty markets or co-ops may carry the blue variety. All can be used interchangeably in recipes, but the yellow variety contains slightly more vitamin A than the others.

2/3 cup milk

3 tablespoons vegetable oil

1 egg

3/4 cup all-purpose flour

3/4 cup cornmeal

2 tablespoons sugar

1 teaspoon baking powder

1/2 teaspoon salt

1 can (8 3/4 ounces) whole kernel corn, drained, or 1 cup frozen (thawed) whole kernel corn

1. Heat oven to 400°. Grease bottoms only of 8 medium muffin cups, 2 1/2 × 1 1/4 inches, or line with paper baking cups.

2. Beat milk, oil and egg in medium bowl. Stir in remaining ingredients except corn just until flour is moistened. Fold in corn. Divide batter evenly among muffin cups (about 3/4 full).

3. Bake 18 to 20 minutes or until golden brown. Immediately remove from pan.

1 Muffin: Calories 190 (Calories from Fat 65); Fat 7g (Saturated 1g); Cholesterol 30mg; Sodium 330mg; Carbohydrate 29g (Dietary Fiber 1g); Protein 4g.

Orange-Currant Muffins

PREP: 15 min; BAKE: 25 min

12 MUFFINS

The secret to making tender muffins is to not overmix the batter. Just stir until all of the flour looks moistened, then gently fold in any remaining ingredients the recipe may call for.

3/4 cup milk

1/3 cup vegetable oil

1/4 cup frozen (thawed) orange juice concentrate

2 teaspoons grated orange peel

1 egg, slightly beaten

2 1/4 cups all-purpose flour

1/2 cup sugar

3 teaspoons baking powder

1/4 teaspoon salt

1/4 cup currants or raisins

3 tablespoons sugar

1 teaspoon grated orange peel

1. Heat oven to 400°. Grease bottoms only of 12 medium muffin cups, 2 1/2 × 1 1/4 inches, or line with paper baking cups.

2. Beat milk, oil, juice concentrate, 2 teaspoons orange peel and the egg in large bowl until blended. Stir in flour, 1/2 cup sugar, the baking powder and salt all at once just until flour is moistened (batter will be lumpy). Fold in currants. Divide batter evenly among muffin cups. Mix 3 tablespoons sugar and 1 teaspoon orange peel; sprinkle over batter in cups.

3. Bake 20 to 25 minutes or until light golden brown. Immediately remove from pan.

1 Muffin: Calories 200 (Calories from Fat 65); Fat 7g (Saturated 1g); Cholesterol 20mg; Sodium 180mg; Carbohydrate 32g (Dietary Fiber 1g); Protein 3g.

Orange-Currant Muffins and Banana-Gingerbread Muffins (page 229)

Cheddar-Cornmeal Scones

PREP: 15 min; BAKE: 25 min

8 SCONES

All-purpose flour comes in bleached and unbleached varieties that can be used interchangeably. Bleaching either occurs naturally through aging or is done chemically. Unbleached flour has a creamier color than bleached flour.

1 1/4 cups all-purpose flour

1 cup cornmeal

1 tablespoon sugar

2 teaspoons baking powder

1/2 teaspoon salt

1/3 cup firm margarine or butter

1/4 cup milk

1 egg, beaten

3/4 cup shredded Cheddar cheese (3 ounces)

1 can (4 ounces) chopped green chilies, undrained

Honey, if desired

1. Heat oven to 425°. Grease cookie sheet.

2. Mix flour, cornmeal, sugar, baking powder and salt in large bowl. Cut in margarine, using pastry blender or crisscrossing 2 knives, until mixture looks like coarse crumbs. Stir in milk, egg, cheese and chilies.

3. Turn dough onto lightly floured surface. Knead lightly 10 times. Pat or roll into an 8-inch circle on cookie sheet. Cut into 8 wedges, but do not separate.

4. Bake 20 to 25 minutes or until golden brown. Immediately remove from cookie sheet; carefully separate wedges. Serve warm with honey.

1 Scone: Calories 240 (Calories from Fat 90); Fat 10g (Saturated 6g); Cholesterol 55mg; Sodium 400mg; Carbohydrate 32g (Dietary Fiber 2g); Protein 7g.

Grains: Selection, Storage and Preparation

SELECTION

Various forms of corn, oats, rice and wheat are widely available in supermarkets. Other grains can be found in the health food section of large supermarkets, in co-ops and health food stores or in specialty mail-order catalogs. Many of these grains are sold in bulk form or are packaged and sold in a refrigerator case. When selecting grains for occasional use, purchase them in small quantities, if possible.

STORAGE

Uncooked Grains

Most grains can be stored indefinitely, but for optimum quality and flavor, we recommend a maximum storage time of one to two years.

- Store in original packaging or transfer to air-tight glass or plastic containers and label contents with starting storage date.

- Store in a cool (60°F or less), dry location. All grains can be refrigerated or frozen, which is a good idea if you live in hot, humid climate. Whole grains that contain oil (brown rice, stone-ground or whole-grain cornmeal, wheat berries, wheat germ and whole wheat flour) can become rancid and *must be stored in the refrigerator or freezer*; store up to six months.

Cooked Grains

- **Refrigerator:** Cooked grains can be covered and stored in the refrigerator for up to five days.

- **Freezer:** Cooked grains can be frozen in air-tight containers for up to six months.

Preparation

Rinsing grains before cooking is not necessary with the exception of quinoa. Grains lose moisture with age, so you may find that you need more or less liquid than the recipe calls for. If all the liquid is absorbed but the grain isn't quite tender, add a little more liquid and cook longer. If it is tender but all the liquid hasn't been absorbed, just drain.

Grains Cooking Chart

Type of Grain (1 cup uncooked amount)	Amount of Cooking Liquid (in cups)	Method of Cooking/ Preparation (using 2-quart saucepan with lid)	Approximate Cooking Time in Minutes	Approximate Yield (in cups)
Arborio	2	Heat liquid to a boil. Stir in rice. Reduce heat. Cover and simmer.	22 to 25	3
Barley (quick-cooking)	2	Heat liquid to a boil. Stir in barley. Reduce heat. Cover and simmer.	10 to 12	3
Barley (regular)	4	Heat liquid to a boil. Stir in barley. Reduce heat. Cover and simmer.	45 to 50	4
Basmati Rice	12 (3 quarts)	Soak in water 30 minutes. Heat rice and liquid to a boil. Boil 5 minutes.		3
Brown Rice	2 3/4	Heat rice and liquid to a boil. Reduce heat. Cover and simmer.	45 to 50	4
Bulgur	3	Pour boiling liquid over bulgur and soak. Do not cook.	Soak 30 to 60 minutes.	3
Couscous	1 1/2	Heat liquid to a boil. Stir in couscous. Cover and remove from heat.	Let stand covered 5 minutes.	3 to 3 1/2
Jasmine and Texmati	1 3/4	Heat rice and liquid to a boil. Reduce heat. Cover and simmer.	15 to 20	3
Kasha (roasted buckwheat kernels)	2	Pour boiling liquid over kasha and soak. Do not cook.	Soak 10 to 15 minutes.	4
Millet	2 1/2	Heat millet and liquid to a boil. Reduce heat. Cover and simmer.	15 to 20	4
Parboiled Rice (converted)	2 1/2	Heat liquid to a boil. Stir in rice. Reduce heat. Cover and simmer.	20 minutes. Remove from heat. Let stand covered 5 minutes.	3 to 4

Type of Grain (1 cup uncooked amount)	Amount of Cooking Liquid (in cups)	Method of Cooking/ Preparation (using 2-quart saucepan with lid)	Approximate Cooking Time in Minutes	Approximate Yield (in cups)
Precooked Brown Rice (instant)	1 1/4	Heat liquid to a boil. Stir in rice. Reduce heat. Cover and simmer.	10 minutes	2
Precooked White Rice (instant)	1	Heat liquid to a boil. Stir in rice. Cover and remove from heat.	Let stand covered 5 minutes.	2
Quinoa	2	Heat quinoa and liquid to a boil. Reduce heat. Cover and simmer.	15	3 to 4
Regular Rice	2	Heat rice and liquid to a boil. Reduce heat. Cover and simmer.	15	3
Wheat Berries	2 1/2	Heat wheat berries and liquid to a boil. Reduce heat. Cover and simmer.	50 to 60	2 3/4 to 3
Wild Rice	2 1/2	Heat rice and liquid to a boil. Reduce heat. Cover and simmer.	40 to 50	3

Lemon and Poppy Seed Scones

PREP: 15 min; BAKE: 15 min

8 SCONES

Currants look like miniature raisins but are actually dried, seedless zante grapes. Currants and raisins can be used interchangeably. For the true lemon lover, you might want to add half a teaspoon grated lemon peel with the currants.

2 cups all-purpose flour

1/4 cup sugar

1 tablespoon poppy seed

3 teaspoons baking powder

1/4 teaspoon salt

1/3 cup firm margarine or butter

1/3 cup currants or raisins

2 tablespoons lemon juice

1 teaspoon grated lemon peel

3/4 cup milk

1. Heat oven to 425°. Spray cookie sheet with cooking spray.

2. Mix flour, sugar, poppy seed, baking powder and salt in large bowl. Cut in margarine, using pastry blender or crisscrossing 2 knives, until mixture looks like fine crumbs. Stir in currants. Mix lemon juice, lemon peel and milk; stir into flour mixture.

3. Turn dough onto lightly floured surface. Knead lightly 10 times. Pat or roll into 9-inch circle on cookie sheet. Brush with milk and sprinkle with sugar if desired. Cut into 8 wedges, but do not separate.

4. Bake 12 to 15 minutes or until golden brown. Immediately remove from cookie sheet; carefully separate wedges. Serve warm.

1 Scone: Calories 240 (Calories from Fat 80); Fat 9g (Saturated 2g); Cholesterol 2mg; Sodium 360mg; Carbohydrate 37g (Dietary Fiber 1g); Protein 4g.

Lemon-Dill Popovers

PREP:15 min; BAKE: 40 min

6 POPOVERS

Popovers are perceived as being difficult to make and high in cholesterol. Wrong on both counts! Try these, and you'll wonder why you never made popovers before.

1 egg plus 2 egg whites
1 cup all-purpose flour
1 cup milk
1/2 teaspoon salt
1/4 teaspoon dried dill weed
1/4 teaspoon grated lemon peel

1. Heat oven to 450°. Generously grease 6-cup popover pan or six 6-ounce custard cups.

2. Beat 1 egg plus 2 egg whites slightly in medium bowl. Beat in remaining ingredients just until smooth (do not overbeat). Fill cups about 1/2 full. Bake 20 minutes.

3. Reduce oven temperature to 350°. Bake about 20 minutes longer or until deep golden brown. Immediately remove from cups. Serve hot.

1 Popover: Calories 100 (Calories from Fat 10); Fat 1g (Saturated 0g); Cholesterol 35mg; Sodium 240mg; Carbohydrate 18g (Dietary Fiber 0g); Protein 5g.

Artichoke-Rosemary Bruschetta

PREP: 10 min; BAKE: 30 min

12 SLICES

Although the saying goes "man cannot live by bread alone," this bread may tempt you to try doing just that! For a terrific meal, try pairing it with a tossed salad loaded with fresh vegetables.

1 loaf (1 pound) French bread, cut horizontally in half
1 cup shredded mozzarella cheese (4 ounces)
1/2 cup grated Parmesan cheese
1 tablespoon chopped fresh or 1 teaspoon dried rosemary leaves, crumbled
2/3 cup mayonnaise or salad dressing
1 jar (6 ounces) marinated artichoke hearts, drained and chopped

1. Heat oven to 375°. Place bread, cut sides up, on ungreased cookie sheet. Bake 10 minutes.

2. Mix 1/2 cup of the mozzarella cheese, the Parmesan cheese, rosemary, mayonnaise and artichokes; spread on bread. Sprinkle with remaining 1/2 cup mozzarella cheese. Bake 15 to 20 minutes or until cheese is melted.

1 Slice: Calories 235 (Calories from Fat 125); Fat 14g (Saturated 3g); Cholesterol 15mg; Sodium 450mg; Carbohydrate 21g (Dietary Fiber 2g); Protein 8g.

Ranch-Parmesan Cheese Toasts

PREP: 8 min; BROIL: 1 min

8 TOASTS

You'll want to try this easy and tasty topping on other breads such as split English muffins, bagels or slices of French bread. When sweet onions are available, such as Vidalia or Walla Walla, you might want to try a thin slice of onion in place of the green onions.

4 hot dog buns, split

1/4 cup ranch dressing

4 medium green onions, chopped (1/3 cup)

1/4 cup grated Parmesan cheese

1. Set oven control to broil. Place buns, cut sides up, on ungreased cookie sheet. Spread dressing on buns. Sprinkle with onions and cheese.

2. Broil with tops 4 to 6 inches from heat about 1 minute or until topping begins to bubble.

1 Toast: Calories 105 (Calories from Fat 45); Fat 5g (Saturated 1g); Cholesterol 5mg; Sodium 230mg; Carbohydrate 12g (Dietary Fiber 0g); Protein 3g.

Southwest Cheese Bread

PREP: 10 min; BAKE: 6 min

8 SLICES

These cheesy bread slices also make great appetizers. After baking, cut each slice into halves or fourths. Top each with a slice of cherry tomato and a piece of fresh cilantro.

8 slices French bread (1/2 inch thick)

1/4 cup mayonnaise or salad dressing

2 tablespoons finely chopped bell pepper

2 tablespoons finely chopped green onion

1 teaspoon chopped fresh cilantro or parsley, if desired

1/2 cup shredded Colby–Jack cheese (2 ounces)

1. Heat oven to 400°.

2. Mix all ingredients except bread and cheese. Spread on one side of each bread slice. Sprinkle with cheese. Place on ungreased cookie sheet.

3. Bake 5 to 6 minutes or until cheese is melted and bread is slightly toasted on bottom.

1 Slice: Calories 150 (Calories from Fat 80); Fat 9g (Saturated 2g); Cholesterol 11mg; Sodium 230mg; Carbohydrate 13g (Dietary Fiber 0g); Protein 4g.

Southwest Cheese Bread

Pesto Mozzarella Loaf

PREP: 10 min; BROIL: 2 min

16 SLICES

Sun-dried tomatoes have an intense tomato flavor as well as some sweet notes that add a lot of flavor wherever they are added. You will find them packaged in dry form or jarred in oil.

1 loaf (1 pound) French bread, cut horizontally in half

1/2 cup pesto

1/2 cup oil-packed sun-dried tomatoes, drained and coarsely chopped, or 1 small tomato, chopped (1/2 cup)

1 cup shredded mozzarella cheese (4 ounces)

1. Set oven control to broil. Place bread, cut sides up, on ungreased cookie sheet. Broil with tops 4 to 6 inches from heat about 1 minute or until lightly toasted.

2. Spread pesto on bread. Sprinkle with tomatoes and cheese. Broil 1 to 2 minutes or until cheese is melted.

1 Slice: Calories 145 (Calories from Fat 65); Fat 7g (Saturated 2g); Cholesterol 5mg; Sodium 270mg; Carbohydrate 16g (Dietary Fiber 1g); Protein 5g.

Sweet Pepper Focaccia

PREP: 10 min; BAKE: 10 min

12 WEDGES

Roma tomatoes, also known as Italian or plum tomatoes, are available in red and yellow varieties. They are oval-shaped and generally smaller in size. Roma tomatoes are ideal for cooking because of their meaty texture and rich flavor.

1 round focaccia bread or Italian bread shell (12 inches in diameter)

1/2 cup finely shredded pizza cheese blend (mozzarella and Cheddar cheeses)

1 small bell pepper, coarsely chopped (1/2 cup)

2 medium roma (plum) tomatoes, chopped (2/3 cup)

2 tablespoons Italian dressing

2 tablespoons grated Parmesan cheese

Shredded fresh basil or oregano leaves, if desired

1. Heat oven to 425°. Place focaccia on ungreased cookie sheet. Sprinkle evenly with pizza cheese blend. Top with bell pepper and tomatoes. Drizzle with dressing.

2. Bake about 10 minutes or until edge of focaccia is golden brown. Sprinkle with Parmesan cheese and basil. Cut into wedges.

1 Wedge: Calories 160 (Calories from Fat 55); Fat 6g (Saturated 1g); Cholesterol 5mg; Sodium 450mg; Carbohydrate 23g (Dietary Fiber 1g); Protein 5g.

14 No-Hassle Meatless Menus

Whether you're a pro at planning meatless meals or just starting out, we're sure you'll find a menu suggestion that will fit your taste and the occasion.

Sunday Brunch

Tex-Mex Scrambled Eggs (page 128)

Corn

Banana-Gingerbread Muffins (page 229)

Assorted Fresh Fruit Platter

Relaxed Saturday Lunch

Warm Tuscan Bean Salad (page 107)

Double Corn Muffins (page 229)

Fresh Fruit

Kids' Favorite Lunch

Super Grilled Cheese Sandwiches (page 64)

Tomato Soup

Carrot and Celery Sticks

Chocolate Cake

Winter Soup Supper

Tortilla Soup (page 19)

Artichoke-Rosemary Bruschetta (page 237)

*Apple Pie with Vanilla Ice Cream
and Warm Caramel Sauce*

Monday Night Football Supper

Italian Grinders (page 58)

Assorted Raw Vegetables

Green and Red Grapes

Banana Splits

Summer Evening Supper

Egg-Asparagus Salad (page 104)

Lemon-Dill Popovers (page 237)

Chocolate Frozen Yogurt

Crisp Sugar Cookies

Friday Night Supper

Easy Vegetable Chow Mein (page 118)

Chow Mein Noodles

Rice

Lime Sherbet

Fortune Cookies

Fix It and Forget It!

Pizza Casserole (page 210)

Romaine Salad

Crusty Italian Bread

Fruit-Flavored Sorbet

Fresh Fruit

Supper on the Deck

Sweet-and-Sour Oriental Pasta Salad (page 94)

Sesame Breadsticks

Minted Iced Tea

Fresh Melon Slices

Kids' Night to Cook

Easy Broccoli Pizza (page 73)

Tossed Salad

Lemonade

Ice-Cream Bars

Good Friends, Good Times

West African Sweet Potato Supper (page 123)

Whole Green Beans

Hearty Multigrain Biscuits (page 228)

Key Lime Pie

Pizza Party

Santa Fe Nacho Pizzas (page 78)

Sun-Dried Tomato and Herb Pizza (page 75)

Tossed Salad

Wine, Beer and Soft Drinks

Frozen Yogurt or Sherbet

Chill-Chasing Chili Get-Together

Three-Bean Enchilada Chili (page 52)

Cheddar-Cornmeal Scones (page 232)

Fresh Orange, Avocado and Onion Salad

Frosted Brownies

Let's Play Cards!

Vegetable Tetrazzini (page 205)

Caesar Salad

Garlic Bread

Bars and Cookies

Going Meatless: A Glossary

Meatless eating is growing in popularity—and it's growing fast! With this new interest, more new and unfamiliar ingredients are popping up in the supermarket, in articles about food and on restaurant menus. The following glossary will help you become more knowledgeable about these new ingredients and foods.

Agar-Agar: A thickening agent made from sea vegetation. It is often used in place of unflavored gelatin, which is made from animal products.

Arborio Rice: Arborio is shorter, fatter and has a higher starch content than regular white rice. Hailing from Italy, this rice is the preferred ingredient in risotto, where its starch contributes to the creamy texture.

Arrowroot: This powdery starch comes from the tropical root of the same name. It is a substitute for unflavored gelatin.

Barley Malt Syrup: A sweetener made from sprouted whole barley. It has a mild caramel flavor and is not as sweet as sugar or honey.

Basmati Rice: A long-grain, finely textured, highly aromatic and nutty-flavored rice. It is often used in Indian and Middle Eastern cuisines.

Brewer's Yeast: This yeast has no leavening power and is used in making beer. It is a good source of vitamin B and is widely used as a nutritional supplement.

Brown Rice Syrup: A cultured sweetener made from brown rice, water and an enzyme. It has a light flavor that is less sweet than sugar.

Carob: Carob is the dried pulp from the pods of the tropical carob tree. It is generally sold ground and used as a substitute for baking cocoa. Carob doesn't contain caffeine.

Chipotle Chilies in Adobo Sauce: Chipotles are smoked jalapeño chilies and are sold either dried or canned in a tomato-based sauce called adobo sauce. They add a rich, smoky, complex flavor to foods.

Cilantro: Also known as Mexican or Chinese parsley or fresh coriander. This herb looks like flat-leaf parsley, but the flavor is very different: strong, fresh and tangy.

Coconut Milk: An unsweetened liquid made from a mixture of coconut flesh that has been steeped in water, then strained. Its consistency can range from thin to quite thick and creamy. It is widely used in Indonesian cuisine.

Cumin: The quintessential flavor in chili con carne and in many popular Tex-Mex and Southwestern foods. It is also used in making curries. Cumin has a strong, warm, complex flavor.

Egg Replacer: Egg replacer is cholesterol-free and is made from starches and leavening ingredients that act similar to fresh eggs. Do not confuse it with cholesterol-free egg substitute products, which are made with egg whites.

Falafel: This Middle-Eastern specialty is a combination of ground garbanzo beans and spices. The mixture is formed into balls or patties and deep-fried, then served in pita bread with a yogurt sauce.

Kelp: Also known as kombu, it is an algae harvested from the ocean. It is available in dried sheets and powdered, a form used as a salt substitute.

Lupini Pasta: A pasta made from the ground beans of the lupin plant, which has been harvested for thousands of years. It contains more protein and fiber than wheat pasta, and because of its low starch content, it doesn't stick together during cooking.

Meat Analogs: Meat substitutes made generally from soybeans and sometimes tofu. They come in many different forms: burgers, sausages, crumbles, hot dogs, ready-made meal mixes (such as chili) and in frozen dinners.

Miso: Is a fermented paste made from soybeans and grain such as barley or rice. Ranging in color from yellow to red to brown, this paste is primarily used as a flavoring ingredient in place of chicken or beef granules.

Nori: Is a seaweed that has been dried in paper-thin sheets. Generally, it is used for wrapping sushi and rice balls.

Seitan: Meat substitute made by combining whole wheat flour and water. After the dough is mixed, it is repeatedly kneaded and rinsed while immersed in water to remove all of its starch. The resulting dough is then simmered in vegetable stock. You can make your own seitan or buy it in many forms.

Soba: Also known as Japanese noodles, soba is made from buckwheat flour and is dark brown in color.

Soy Cheese: Is made from tofu or soy milk and tastes similar to cheese made with cow's milk. Although soy cheeses do contain fat, they are cholesterol free.

Soy Milk: Is made by pressing ground cooked soybeans. It is higher in protein than cow's milk. Because it's a nondairy product, it's a common substitute for those with milk allergies.

Soy Yogurt: Is made from cultured soy milk and is available in many flavors. Soy yogurt is lactose-free and cholesterol-free.

Tahini: Also known as sesame seed paste, it comes from the Middle East and is made from ground sesame seeds. It is the critical ingredient in hummus, a classic Middle-Eastern dip of pureed garbanzo beans.

Tamari: This soybean product is very similar in flavor to soy sauce, but it is more subtle and a little bit thicker.

Tempeh: Is made from fermented soybeans. It has a chewy texture and a mild flavor similar to fresh mushrooms. It is available flavored and unflavored in refrigerated and frozen forms.

Texturized Soy Protein (also known as TSP): TSP is soy flour that has been compressed until the protein fibers change in structure. It is available in a dried granular form and requires rehydration. It has a texture similar to ground beef. It can be used to replace part or all of the ground meat in some recipes. Chunk-size pieces also are available to replace stew meat.

Tofu: Also known as soybean curd or bean curd, tofu is made from soybeans. The soybeans are soaked, cooked, ground and then mixed with a curdling ingredient. The resulting curds are drained and pressed into cakes, which are tofu. It is very mildly flavored with a taste similar to a very mild cheese. Because it is so mild, it easily absorbs the flavors of the herbs, spices and foods it is cooked with.

STOCK OPTIONS: THE VEGETARIAN PANTRY

Going vegetarian or meatless? Now is the time to consider what to stock in your pantry, refrigerator and freezer to make meal preparation easier. This list is just a beginning; we're sure you will add your own favorites to it, as well.

On the Shelf

Canned whole beans: black, butter, cannellini, great northern, kidney, navy, pinto

Canned vegetarian baked, chili and refried beans

Canned or jarred sauces: chutney, mustards, pasta sauces, pesto, relishes, salsa

Canned vegetarian soups and broth

Canned tomato products: plain and seasoned

Dried fruit: apricots, dates, diced dried fruits, raisins

Dried legumes: beans, lentils, split peas

Nuts: almonds, cashews, peanuts, pecans, sunflower nuts, walnuts

Peanut butter

Spices and herbs

Texturized soy protein (TSP) mixes (chili, sloppy joes, soup)

Grains: barley, oats, rice, roasted buckwheat groats—also known as kasha

Pasta

Prebaked pizza crusts or shells

Ready-to-eat cereals

Whole grain breads and rolls

Whole grain crackers

In the Refrigerator

Fresh vegetables

Fresh fruit

Cheeses

Milk

Yogurt

Hummus

Fresh herbs

Flour and corn tortillas

In the Freezer

Meat substitutes: vegetable burgers, vegetarian hot dogs and breakfast meats

Cheese or vegetable pizza

Fruit and vegetable juices

Fruits

Vegetables

Metric Conversion Guide

Volume

U.S. Units	Canadian Metric	Australian Metric
1/4 teaspoon	1 mL	1 ml
1/2 teaspoon	2 mL	2 ml
1 teaspoon	5 mL	5 ml
1 tablespoon	15 mL	20 ml
1/4 cup	50 mL	60 ml
1/3 cup	75 mL	80 ml
1/2 cup	125 mL	125 ml
2/3 cup	150 mL	170 ml
3/4 cup	175 mL	190 ml
1 cup	250 mL	250 ml
1 quart	1 liter	1 liter
1 1/2 quarts	1.5 liters	1.5 liters
2 quarts	2 liters	2 liters
2 1/2 quarts	2.5 liters	2.5 liters
3 quarts	3 liters	3 liters
4 quarts	4 liters	4 liters

Weight

U.S. Units	Canadian Metric	Australian Metric
1 ounce	30 grams	30 grams
2 ounces	55 grams	60 grams
3 ounces	85 grams	90 grams
4 ounces (1/4 pound)	115 grams	125 grams
8 ounces (1/2 pound)	225 grams	225 grams
16 ounces (1 pound)	455 grams	500 grams
1 pound	455 grams	1/2 kilogram

Note: The recipes in this cookbook have not been developed or tested using metric measures. When converting recipes to metric, some variations in quality may be noted.

Measurements

Inches	Centimeters
1	2.5
2	5.0
3	7.5
4	10.0
5	12.5
6	15.0
7	17.5
8	20.5
9	23.0
10	25.5
11	28.0
12	30.5
13	33.0

Temperatures

Fahrenheit	Celsius
32°	0°
212°	100°
250°	120°
275°	140°
300°	150°
325°	160°
350°	180°
375°	190°
400°	200°
425°	220°
450°	230°
475°	240°
500°	260°

Helpful Nutrition and Cooking Information

Nutrition Guidelines:

We provide nutrition information for each recipe that includes calories, fat, cholesterol, sodium, carbohydrate, fiber and protein. Individual food choices can be based on this information

Recommended intake for a daily diet of 2,000 calories as set by the Food and Drug Organization

Total Fat	Less than 65g
Saturated Fat	Less than 20g
Cholesterol	Less than 300mg
Sodium	Less than 2,400mg
Total Carbohydrate	300g
Dietary Fiber	25g

Criteria Used for Calculating Nutrition Information:

- The first ingredient was used wherever a choice is given (such as 1/3 cup sour cream or plain yogurt).

- The first ingredient amount was used wherever a range is given (such as 3 to 3 1/2 pound cut-up broiler-fryer chicken).

- The first serving number was used wherever a range is given (such as 4 to 6 servings).

- "If desired" ingredients (such as sprinkle with brown sugar if desired) and recipe variations were *not* included .

- Only the amount of a marinade or frying oil that is estimated to be absorbed by the food during preparation or cooking was calculated.

Cooking Terms Glossary:

Beat: Mix ingredients vigorously with spoon, fork, wire whisk, hand beater or electric mixer until smooth and uniform.

Boil: Heat liquid until bubbles rise continuously and break on the surface and steam is given off. For rolling boil, the bubbles form rapidly.

Chop: Cut into coarse or fine irregular pieces with a knife, food chopper, blender or food processor.

Cube: Cut into squares 1/2 inch or larger.

Dice: Cut into squares smaller than 1/2 inch.

Grate: Cut into tiny particles using small rough holes of grater (citrus peel or chocolate).

Grease: Rub the inside surface of a pan with shortening, using pastry brush, piece of waxed paper or paper towel, to prevent food from sticking during baking (as for some casseroles).

Julienne: Cut into thin, matchlike strips, using knife or food processor (vegetables, fruits, meats).

Mix: Combine ingredients in any way that distributes them evenly.

Sauté: Cook foods in hot oil or margarine over medium-high heat with frequent tossing and turning motion.

Shred: Cut into long thin pieces by rubbing food across the holes of a shredder, as for cheese, or by using a knife to slice very thinly, as for cabbage.

Simmer: Cook in liquid just below the boiling point on top of the stove; usually after reducing heat from a boil. Bubbles will rise slowly and break just below the surface.

Stir: Mix ingredients until uniform consistency. Stir once in a while for stirring occasionally, often for stirring frequently and continuously for stirring constantly.

Toss: Tumble ingredients lightly with a lifting motion (such as green salad), usually to coat evenly or mix with another food.

Ingredients Used in Recipe Testing and Nutrition Calculations:

- Ingredients used for testing represent those that the majority of consumers use in their homes: large eggs, 2% milk, 80% lean ground beef, canned ready-to-use chicken broth, and vegetable oil spread containing *not less than 65% fat.*

- Fat-free, low-fat or low-sodium products are not used, unless otherwise indicated.

- Solid vegetable shortening (not butter, margarine, nonstick cooking sprays or vegetable oil spread as they can cause sticking problems) is used to grease pans, unless otherwise indicated.

Equipment Used in Recipe Testing:

We use equipment for testing that the majority of consumers use in their homes. If a specific piece of equipment (such as a wire whisk) is necessary for recipe success, it will be listed in the recipe.

- Cookware and bakeware **without** nonstick coatings were used, unless otherwise indicated.

- No dark colored, black or insulated bakeware was used.

- When a baking *pan* is specified in a recipe, a *metal* pan was used; a baking *dish* or pie *plate* means oven-proof glass was used.

- An electric hand mixer was used for mixing *only when mixer speeds are specified* in the recipe directions. When a mixer speed is not given, a spoon or fork was used.

Index

Numbers in *italics* refer to photos.